365 Daily

Angel Messages
from Your Angels

for Healing, Inspiration and Guidance

Angel Lady Terrie Marie, D.Ms.

About the Author

Terrie Marie, D.Ms., the Angel Whisperer, is an Amazon Best-Selling Author who has an *Unusual and Highly Effective* way of showing Heart-Centered Women and Men how to show-up more powerfully in their life, work and business when they access their Ultimate Angel Dream Team.

Angel Lady Terrie Marie *specializes in showing her clients how to directly access and receive Divine Guidance through their Higher-Self and Angels*, raise your inner vibration, your Divine Wealth Frequency, change thought patterns, enhance the Law of Attraction and magnify your manifesting power.

She helps you *discover, explore and learn practical, easy-to-use techniques*, tips and tools to increase prosperity and abundance with more harmony and less stress. The Angel Lady shows you how to *trust your intuition and gut feelings* with a heightened sense of empowerment and confidence.

Her subtle, *powerful insights create life-changing transformations from the inside out.* Terrie Marie has helped Heart and Soul-Centered women and men in Australia, South Africa, Ghana, New Zealand, Germany, Belgium, Canada, United Kingdom, Mexico, Brazil, Sweden and the United States.

Terrie Marie, D.Ms. has the unique ability to *connect and communicate with Angels* which makes her a highly sought after Angel Mentor and Angel Whisperer.

When the Angel Lady is being interviewed or speaking to International audiences, her *high energy ignites the atmosphere with her empowering message*, her unconditional love shines bright and intuitive insights flow through her. She creates Sacred Space to *transform goals and dreams into reality.*

Day 1

NEW BEGINNINGS
Guardian Angel of New Beginnings

~*~

Tis the day the Lord hath made.
How shall you honor the child within?
How shall you nurture all that is within you this day? The spark of
Divinity within yearns to be expressed
The spark of Divinity within yearns to be nurtured with love.
Plant the seeds of your desires, tend them, weed out the ego voice, water
these precious seeds with light and love, visions of comple-
tion...remembering to rejoice along the journey.
Go forth, plant the seeds of your inner most desires ... delight in the
growth before you this day.

Day 2

FLOATING IN THE SEA OF DIVINE LOVE
Guardian Angel of the South

Imagine a lake or the ocean ... close your eyes ... see beautiful blues or
greens, the most beautiful colors you can imagine.
The intensity of color is beyond anything you have ever seen ... you are
perfectly safe, yes, even if this is the very first time your physical body has
been in a lake or the ocean.
Imagine you are floating in a beautiful lake or the ocean ... how does it
feel to know, absolutely know you are supported in every way?
The water is very gently caressing your physical body.
Perhaps you feel as though all your cares or worries are washed away by
the gentle motion of the water as you gently float in complete surrender.
What would it feel like to have all your earthly desires fulfilled?
What would it feel like to have all your emotional, physical, and spiritual
desires fulfilled?
There is only peace and harmony in the Sea of Divine Love.
There is only light in the Sea of Divine Love.
There is only healing in the Sea of Divine Love.
There is only love in the Sea of Divine Love.
The Lord Creator, Divine Source Energy is all there is.

Day 3

ANGELS SURROUND YOU

Angels are all around you this very moment ... if you will take a moment
to breathe deeply, exhaling slowly ... do you not feel a sense of calming
peace?

How then can Angels not be with you in this moment and the next and
the next?

Is there something or someone you wish to bring into your experience
this day?

How will you know or recognize the manifestation of that which you
desire?

This we say to you ... being in a state of joy ... giving of yourself to the
self and to others ... appreciate all that surrounds you.

In what way will you choose to be in the moment, celebrating all that is
positive in your life?

Day 4

DIVINE BIRTHRIGHT
Angel of Divine Connection

⌒✍⌒

We ask this of you ... ponder if you will the true essence of who you are.
Not just the physicalness of the existence perceived as reality but the
true essence of your being both physical and non-physical.
Remember your connection to Divine Source Energy, the inner essence
of what you call your soul.
Reach within, past the hurts and sorrows of the earthly realm.
If only in this one moment, remember who you are. Let all else fall from
your shoulders, from your thoughts, from your heart.
There is only love and light.
The shear essence of your being, is light and love from the Divine.
Your Divine birthright is the key to all that is before you ... love
happiness, joy, peace, calm and harmony. How shall you choose to claim
that which already is?

Day 5

TRANQUILITY
Angel of Tranquility

⌒✕⌒

Imagine you are standing on the shore of a big sapphire blue lake; there
are trees all along the shore of this beautiful sapphire blue lake.
The lake is so peaceful, the surface is a smooth as silk, and not even one
small ripple disturbs the peace and tranquility of the lake.
Take a few moments to really see this beautiful, peaceful lake.
Imagine you are floating, safely and contentedly, floating in the sapphire
blue lake.
You float effortlessly without a care; there is only peace and tranquility.
Sense the bliss.
Sense peace and joy as the sapphire blue lake gently cradles you.
Return to this place as often as you choose.
Return to this place, experience peace and tranquility, reconnecting
with Divine Source Energy.

Day 6

TRANSFORMATION
Angel of Divine Connection

⁓Ɱ⁓

Divine love is all there is.
Divine love is all there is in the Realm of Spirit and harmony.
Divine love is all there is.
Divine love is the connection between what is and what is to be.
Divine love is a gift freely given to you by Divine Source ... the source of
all light and love.
Divine love transforms all thought, all emotion, all action into light.
There is only light.
There is only love.
Divine Love is all there is.

Day 7

FLOAT IN TOTAL SURRENDER
Angel of Surrender

Float in total surrender as you ponder for a moment the question before
you. What do you long for?
Where in your life experience do you perceive lack? Lack as defined in
the Earthly Realm is the absence of that which you desire. Perceived lack
is from thoughts of fear, fear of not having ... fear of not being ... fear of
being less than.
Any thought, emotion or action that is not based in love ... love of the
self, loving thoughts towards yourself and others ... is an attempt by the
ego to distract you from all that is. There is only love.
Imagine for a few moments floating effortlessly in a fluffy white cloud
Angels are all around you.
Float in the cloud ... feel the softness ... feel loving energy all around and
within you. Feel every thought, every emotion fall from you. Float in
total surrender.
We are not suggesting you give all away.
We are suggesting you float in total serenity.
Float in total surrender that all is well, all is in Divine Order floating in
total surrender with an open heart and an open mind.
Open yourself to Divine Source Energy.
Open yourself to your true essence, to your connection with all there is.
Float in total surrender allowing Divine Love and Light to flow through
you and around you illuminating every cell in your physical being
projecting outward touching all you come into contact with this
moment and the next and the next. Surrender fear for it is not rooted in
love ... it is not rooted in light ... float in total surrender.

Day 8

WALKING THE PATH OF LIGHT
Angel of Illumination

Walking the Path of Light one must rise above confusion seeing the path before them illuminated with Light and Love ... seeing and sensing your right path.

See Divine Light shine into every place within and around you this moment.

There is only light there is only love ... all perception of shadow or darkness is fully illuminated with light. All is revealed in the light ... light is a Divine Gift freely given to you by Divine Source.

Honor your inner voice. Honor your inner sight.

Trust what you see and hear is truth, your truth. Become quiet ... breathe in light ... breathe out shadow or darkness ... breathe in light ... breathe out shadow or darkness.

Deep within you know the way. You know the right path for you. You know that which is for your highest and best good ... trust.

Walking the path of light need not be other than fully illuminated with love and light.

How shall you choose to walk the path before you this day?

Day 9

ETERNAL RADIANCE
Angel of Radiance

The light of Divine Source shines forth from within you and through
you, radiating outward like a beacon of light.
You are a beacon of light for your Self and for all others who care to see
the Light of the Divine.
Close your eyes.
Do you not see light radiating from Divine Source? How then can you
not see the Divine Source radiating from your physical being?
You are a beloved child filled with Light and Love beyond measure.
The Spirit ... the Soul ... know beyond words, the Light of the Divine is
beyond measure, for the Light is eternally radiant.
There is no darkness, there is only light ... the Light of Eternal Radiance
shines forth from within you.

Day 10

BALANCE EARTH AND SPIRIT
Archangel Metatron

Balance in all things earthly. Balance in all things spiritual.
How does one attain balance when at first it appears there are so many
who experience lack?
Lack is the perception of not having enough time, enough money, a
better job, or not having the right person to share your life.
Lack is another name for fear ... balance your inner Spirit with Earthly
desires. Balance your inner spirit with Spiritual Growth.
We ask you ponder for a few moments gifting your Self with time. Gift
your Self with loving words. Gift another with words, thoughts and acts
of kindness without regard for return.
In what way or ways will you choose to balance the Earthly Realm with
the Spiritual Realm, both of which reside within you this moment?
Balance can be as simple as taking a deep breath, calming yourself ...
passing along your smile to another... giving a moment of our time
especially when it appears there is so little time to share with your Self.
All is freely given by Divine Source. Why then, should what is freely
given be held from you or held from another?
Give freely for it is freely given.

Day 11

BECOME STILL
Guardian Angel of Spiritual Growth

⌒✎⌒

Your Spiritual Self is that part of you which flows through physical
realm experiences, remembering your connection to Divine Source.
We ask you remain open, flowing easily and gracefully with all of life
both physical and ethereal.
There are no mistakes, there are no coincidences.... things only co -
incide coming together, flowing one into the other.
There may be moments in which you find yourself experiencing dis-
satisfaction with or about situations around you. That which is
occurring around or perhaps within you, is often perceived as reality in
the earthly realm.
As you walk the path opening before you, become still. Breathe. See.
Hear. Is this really what you are choosing to experience in this moment?
We ask you remember you are always aligned with Divine Source. With
each step along the path before you, with each healing experience you
become more spiritually aligned with you who truly are ... a beloved
child of Divine Source capable of manifesting all you desire, for there is
only abundance and prosperity in all forms manifesting before you each
moment.
How shall you choose to experience the path before you this moment
and the next and the next?
Will you choose to flow in joy and harmony.

Day 12

CHOICE
Angel Prince of the East

⌒*Ж*⌒

Each and every moment brings with it the opportunity to choose love or fear. To choose what you do want rather than what do you do not want. There are many choices made within each moment. Whatever is before you this moment, we encourage you to become still, breathe deeply calming your conscious mind, calming that which appears to be out of balance.

Open your mind and heart to the possibility of seeing through the eyes of love ... seeing the situation or perceived challenge through a softened gaze. Consider viewing the situation or challenge before you from a different perspective. Adjust your physical gaze just off-center allowing the edges of the image to become slightly out of focus.

What do you see? Take a few moments to really see. How shall you choose to see that which is before you in this moment ... that which is different than the moment that has come before.

You have the freedom to choose differently in the next moment. Having chosen; honor the choice knowing a different choice can be made in the next moment and the next.

There is no right or wrong choice, there is only this moment. How shall you choose to travel the path before you this day?

Day 13

SMOOTH HARMONIOUS TRANSITION
Archangel Jeremiel

Archangel Jeremiel shares his gifts for smooth, harmonious transitions.
Imagine if you will the deepest eggplant purple, rich, vibrant ... so purple
it is nearly black.
Wrap your Self within the richness of Jeremiel's vibrant, gentle energy.
With the passing of each moment there is a choice of holding on to
what has come before or that which is before you.
All is in Divine Order.
Choosing to be calm and harmonious as you travel along the path before
you unfolds easily and harmoniously. There is much joy in releasing that
which no longer serves your highest and best good. Be kind to you as
you review what has come before, making way for what is before you.
How shall you choose to journey through this time of change? Choose
that which resonates within you; align your energy centers ... meditate
... breathe deeply releasing any perceived shadow or darkness ... if you
wish, light a purple candle, offering prayer to calm the way before you.
Gentleness is a most precious gift. Gentleness is loving guidance.
Gentleness is taking time for you and those around you. Gentleness is
speaking from the heart, with loving kindness. Gentleness is.
Be gentle with you this day.

Day 14

BEAUTY
Archangel Jophiel

~*~

There is much beauty within you. There is much beauty in all that
surrounds you.
See through the eyes of beauty and beauty will manifest in your life.
Speak from the heart with love. Reaching inward, speak with
compassion and love.
Wounding another only serves to wound your Inner-Self, your Spirit.
We do not ask you deny that which is conceived in fear. We simply ask
that you choose to see the beauty in that which is before you.
Choose to speak with compassion to you and those around you. Choose
to see kindness. Choose to see through Divine Love and Light ... all is
made manifest in beauty, love and light.
Surround yourself with loving energy, light candles to brighten the way.
Reach out to those who will assist you in manifesting that which you
desire, to guide and support you along the path before you.
There is always a choice between beauty or that of shadow and darkness.
Is the way not more joyous when traveling in the loving energy of beauty
and joy?
How shall you choose this day?

Day 15

HARMONY AND BALANCE
Archangel Haniel

Light a silver candle meditate upon the flame, centering mind, body and spirit.
Feel a sense of calm wash over you, within you and around you.
Feel all troubles and worries fall away from you. Peace and serenity fill your entire being body, mind and soul.
Breathe in light ... exhale shadow and darkness ... breathe in the light of Divine Source.
See beauty in all there is. See beauty within.
In all you do there is harmony and balance.
In the silence know all is in Divine Order. In the silence know all is perfectly ordered.
Harmony and balance are yours for the accepting. Receive the gift that is already yours.
Grace, beauty, inner wisdom and strength are already a part of your inner being. Find what you seek first within, that which you desire shall be made manifest in the outer, physical realm.
See you as whole, complete and perfect.
See through the eyes of Divine Source and that of Angels.

Day 16

ANGELIC PROTECTION
Archangel Michael

Call upon Archangel Michael for protection against all that is not of love, truth, justice, or integrity. Surround you with Light and Love of Divine Source. Ask Archangel Michael to cleanse away all lower energies from your home, work, physical, mental, emotional and spiritual bodies.

What is before you this moment? What situation or possible situation faces you this moment? Archangel Michael reminds us to call upon him for protection both in the physical realm and the Realm of Spirit.

His mighty Sword pierces through all perceived shadow or darkness, negativity, all attachments real or perceived of those who would attempt to draw energy from you.

Call upon Archangel Michael, whispering his name three times. See that which faces you now, this moment cleansed of all impurity, cleansed of all that is based in fear. See that which faces you as healed in harmony, peace and light. See that which faces you, simply dissolve before you, wrapped in a cocoon of pure white light, floating into the Light for healing and transmutation.

There is nothing to fear, there is only Love and Light. Go in peace, journey the path before you in peace and harmony this day and the next. There is none who dare harm a beloved Divine Source.

Day 17

VIBRATIONAL ENERGY
Archangel Raphael

⌇

There is hope. There is faith.
Your source for all things is Divine Source.
It matters not the name by which you seek to strengthen your
connection with the keeper and giver of all that is.
Only that which is thought to be lost is lost. That which is known to be
made manifest is made manifest.
Be watchful of your vibration ... thoughts, actions, emotions ... words
spoken.
Imagine if you will the color purple. What thought or emotion comes to
mind?
Imagine the color brown. What thought or emotion comes to mind?
Each color, thought, emotion, action ... each word spoken carries its
own unique vibrational energy. Choose all with love and compassion.
Speak kindly to you and to others.
That which you truly are, resonates deep within you.
Open your heart and your mind to the light of all there is.
Shine forth this day, casting away all appearance of shadow or darkness
for there is only light this day and the next.

Day 18

PURIFICATION
Archangel Taharial

⌒⁘⌒

White symbolizes purity, integrity, the Light of Divine Source.
Brilliant white Light cleanses and purifies all things, all thoughts, all
emotions...take a few moments, get comfortable, breathe deeply holding
the breath ... exhale slowly. Breathe in ... hold... exhale ... breathe in..
hold... exhale ... imagine your Crown Chakra opening to Divine Source.
Archangel Taharial is by your side.
You are enfolded in his magnificent wings of pure white light.
Archangel Taharial's light is so bright he is nearly translucent.
See sparkles of shimmering light.
See this brilliant white luminescent light enter your Crown Chakra,
gently flowing through your body all the way down to your toes.
See or *sense* this beautiful light filling your entire physical being and your
Aura energy field ... your body begins to glow.
All that is not of light is cleansed and purified.
There is a beautiful rainbow just in front you.
Reach out to touch the gift of total alignment ... breathe in all the colors
of the rainbow.
How do you feel?
You have the power to return in any moment.
Travel this day enfolded in a cocoon of brilliant white light.

Day 19

SEEK AND YOU SHALL FIND
Archangel Zadkiel

⁓✐⁓

The power of Divine Source is great. What do you of Divine Source this
day?
Do you seek peace, harmony or perhaps more joy and less judgment
upon you or others?
What do you choose to call to you this day?
The Mercy of Divine Source is unconditional. The Righteousness of
Divine Source is unconditional. The love of Divine Source is
unconditional.
There is only that which already is. There is only peace. There is
harmony.
There is only joy. There is nothing else.
This day, we ask you consider prayer, meditation, the lighting of candles,
sitting in the silence to better know you.
In better knowing you, you strengthen your connection to that of
Divine Source.
Ahhh the question then becomes ... if you are always connected to the
One, then how can you strengthen something that already is?
In being a part of the physical realm it is possible to experience dis-
connection from Source. Dis-connection appears in many forms.
The ego-chitter chatter barks mightily, creating the perception that
there is only the voice of dis-content, the voice of dis-ease, the voice of
lack.
There is always choice.
How do you choose to walk upon the path this day?

Day 20

JOURNEY OF TRANSITION
Archangel Ariel

There are many facets of being in the physical realm, appreciating the
path along the journey.
Know the journey represents the path before you.
There are many choices, the appearance of distractions along the way.
Earth Mother and Father Sky are in constant renewal; is it not also
possible for you to be in a state of constant renewal.
Perhaps you have recently experienced a transition unlike any other ... a
Dark Night of the Soul before the dawning.
As Earth Mother strives to renew the cycle of transition, you have the
choice of releasing into the light all that has come before this moment.
The gift of transition brings with it the transmutation or the release of
what has come before, cleansing and purifying the physical, emotional
and spiritual bodies.
Honor you, honor Earth Mother and Father Sky, honor all that has
come before, honor this moment and all that is before you.

Day 21

FOCUSED THOUGHT
Archangel Uriel

⌒*w*⌒

Focused thought ... prayer requests released to the Light ... in what way
do you focus your thoughts, emotions ... your vibration manifesting
your heart's desire?
We ask this of you ... make a commitment to you this moment ...
breathe in the Light and the Fire of Divine Source. Exhale all perceived
fear of the unknown.
Breathe in the Light and Fire of Divine Source.
Exhale surrendering the fear of not having that which you desire most.
Take pen to hand, create the vision you most desire for the journey
before you.
We ask you conceive without limitation, we ask you conceive with
abundance and prosperity....there is no limitation. There is no lack in
the Realm of Source.
Do you wish a deeper spiritual understanding of your life's purpose in
the physical realm?
Do you wish prosperity? Do you wish freedom from limiting thoughts?
Do you desire a more harmonious, loving relationship with the one by
your side?
Do you desire the right and perfect life mate?
Take pen to hand; create all that you desire knowing all is already given
you in the moment of the asking.
Ask Archangel Uriel for his hand in manifesting your heart's desires,
knowing you will be shown the way.
Trust this is so ... this or something better.
Begin to give thanks for the manifestation of all you desire and more.

Day 22

GRATITUDE
Archangel Chamuel

Begin each day in gratitude for that which faces you is in Divine Order.
Begin giving thanks to Divine Source for all blessings great and small.
Blessings given or received manifest as gifts of time, love, support,
compassion, acceptance, abundance, enlightenment.
A gift given to the Self is a gift given to all in the physical realm.
Peace and harmony, compassion and acceptance, love and forgiveness,
prosperity and abundance.
Begin each day in gratitude, all is in Divine Order. Accept you, accept
others.
You are a beloved child of Divine Source.
Wash your Spirit with unconditional love. Wash your spirit in the Light
of the Flame of Divine Source.
Begin each day in gratitude.

Day 23

INNER PEACE
Archangel Zaphiel

✒

Open your heart. Open your mind to all that is. Open your heart.
Open your mind to that which has come before.
Light a pale blue candle.
Call upon Archangel Zaphiel filling your heart with softness, filling
your heart with forgiveness, filling your heart with Divine Love and
Light.
Let not the ego speak for you.
Let not the ego direct your ways.
Let not the ego distract you.
Inner peace is a knowing, a knowing which fills your Soul, defining your
very essence. There is only love in this place, know this to be your truth
for there is only light there is only love.
Doubt and fear have no place where inner peace and harmony reign.
Travel this day in peace and harmony.

Day 24

BE OPEN TO THAT WHICH IS ALREADY YOURS
Angel Gadiel

There is a stirring within you this moment ... what first comes to mind?
Do you wish to transform your life? Do you wish to release limiting
beliefs?
Do you seek assistance in maintaining a most loving, judgment free
sense of you and others as you travel the journey before you?
Whichever you choose in seeking assistance, know Angel Gadiel is by
your side for the asking.
Light a yellow candle, feel a slight breeze play upon your skin. Close
your eyes ... breathe deeply; exhaling slowly.... there is much love within
you this moment.
There is much love in all that surrounds you. Take solace for there is
much to celebrate along the journey in the realm of the physical senses.
There is much to release as there will always be those who would seek to
destroy that which you hold closest to your heart.
Take heed ... hold Sacred that which is your truth. Hold Sacred that
which radiates from your heart center.
Hold the vision of that which you desire most. Hold the vision for
others in time of great need.
Hold the vision of peace and harmony. Hold the vision of great love for
all humankind. Hold the vision of abundance for there is surely enough
for all.
Release all thoughts, emotions, actions, perceived hurt.
In the releasing of all, there is great joy. Rejoice for all is yours for the
asking.
Be open to receiving that which you are wanting. Be open to that which
you are asking.

Day 25

SPEAKING ONE'S TRUTH
Archangel Gabriel

⟨⟩

This is the day the Lord hath made. Go in peace, love, harmony and joy.
That which is before you is a truth for you for as long as a breath shall be
sustained. That which is before you, has already begun to pass.
All that has come before this moment delivered you to that place in
which you find you. Breathe deeply beloved child of Divine Source.
Breathe deeply; breathe in the light and love of Divine Source. Fill your
lungs with the power and glory of all that is. Exhale slowly; exhale
completely returning to the light that which attempts to mis-direct you
away from Divine Source and your own Divinity. Speaking one's truth is
essential as you journey the path before you.
Speaking truth with love, illuminating darkness with Creator's light
elevates your vibration and all around you.
Speaking a truth in the physical realm is cause for celebration regardless
of outwardly appearances.
Speaking truth empowers, shedding light into that which is being
portrayed as truth. Know that I am with you always.
Beloved Child of Light are a messenger casting away shadow, casting
away doubt and fear. As you journey the path before you, know you are
never alone.
In speaking truth, light is shed where darkness attempts to prevail.
All is in Divine Order. Know this to be true for there is only Light, there
is only Love. Raise your Spirit to the Source of All There Is, know you
are loved.
Faith, harmony and joy shall sustain you.

HONORING YOUR INNER VOICE
Angel of Discernment

Discernment is a knowing ... a knowing in choosing to honor your inner voice.

A knowing resonates from within. There is no mistaking that which is yours to do.

The path before you may appear to be wrought with peril, consequences unforeseen. Discernment is knowing, speaking one's truth can be the road less traveled.

Learning to discern truth from illusion is developing keen insight and loving judgment, pondering the way in which you choose to travel the path before you.

How does one awaken the gift of discernment?

Be willing to open your heart and your mind.

Be willing to hear your own inner guidance. The asking is all that is necessary to open you to all that is.

Trust that which you receive is Divine Guidance from Creator.

Become quiet, release all thoughts. Breathe deeply ... exhale slowly ... as your mind wanders, gently guide it back to the sweet silence of nothingness.

It is in the silence you will hear, you will feel or sense that which is for your highest and best good knowing all is in Divine Order.

What is before you this moment? What choices face you?

Know Angels are by your side in all moments guiding and protecting all who share the journey.

Day 27

KNOW PEACE AND HARMONY
Archangel Raguel

Be kind to you and to others.
Be charitable to you and to others.
Kindness and Charity are gifts both given and received.
Open to receive the gift of peace and harmony.
Open to receive the gift of joy and happiness.
Open to receive the gift of abundance and prosperity.
All gifts are freely given by Divine Source.
Unconditional love, unconditional light ... all is freely given.
In the accepting is also the giving, for all is in Divine Order.
Know peace and harmony.
Know joy.
Open to receive.

Day 28

ANGELIC GUIDANCE
Archangel Sariel

Before the dawning of day is the gateway between the Heavens and the Earthly Realm. In the land of in-between, lay the dreams and hopes of what lay before you.

By the light of the moon speak your dreams; listen for the sound of silence in the coolness of the night skies.

You who seek guidance through the Realm of Dreams, what symbols have been given to you?

There is nothing to fear in the gateway between the Heavens and the Earthly Realm for there is only peace, love, and light ... the Light of Divine Source.

What dreams speak from within you?

Do you desire a smoother transition from this moment to where you choose to be?

Do you desire different thoughts or actions to guide your way?

Speak your dreams to you keeping all Sacred within your heart.

In the silence lay the guidance you seek.

Travel this day in peace and harmony.

Day 29

OFFER NON-RESISTANCE
Angel of Serenity

⌒⁓

There are many pebbles along the path you travel each day.
Some would seek to distract, to shatter faith and trust.
Some would seek to discourage, entangling you in a web of deceit or
confrontation. There is much which softens each footstep along the
way, cushioning that which is before you.
In all things there is a choice of peace and serenity or resistance and dis-
harmony. There are many manifestations of all that is before you.
The pebbles are symbolic of Earthly Realm challenges.
We ask you ponder for a moment offering non-resistance to that which
is before you.
Is it not possible to allow the flow of something without offering
resistance to it? Offering non-resistance is much like floating along on a
river. The current will loving escort you to your destination.
There is always the choice of traveling in the opposite direction, causing
great struggle or resistance.
If you do not like the direction in which you are traveling or flowing,
offer a different vibration; change your thoughts, emotions or actions.
Changing the way you see things, changes the things you see.
In offering non-resistance to that which has already come before, opens
the way before you, to that which you truly desire. That which is not for
your highest and best good simply falls from you.
In all things seek the path of least resistance. Seeing through the eyes of
love does not mean you must accept the negativity of others. Instead we
suggest you acknowledge and move through in peace and harmony for
that which is resisted is attracted to your vibration.

Offering non-resistance is a most loving gift to you.
Allow the flow of Divine Source Energy to guide you this day.

Day 30

KNOW YOUR SELF
Archangel Raziel

Dear Beloved child of Divine Source, know your beauty.
Know your soul.
Know Divine Source, I and my brethren are by your side.
There is no desire too great or too small.
There is nothing beyond your grasp. What is it you choose?
How do you choose to travel the path along the journey before you?
Know you are a Beloved Child of the Universe.
See beyond the physical realm into that of Spirit.
Can you not see the Light of Divine Source dwells within you?
As you step into darkness, hold the lantern before you.
See the Light shine forth into every place and into everything.
How then can there be darkness or shadow when there is only Light?
Call upon Archangel Raziel and all shall be revealed to you.
What do you wish to manifest within you that then manifests around
you in physical form?
What do you wish to manifest in the outer, physical realm?
Choose wisely, for all you request is made manifest at your choosing.

Day 31

COMMUNICATION WITH THE SELF
Angel Ambriel

Communicating desires of the Soul, from the heart may at first appear as challenges filled with fear.

Speaking one's truth from the heart through the Soul can seek to release the Self from all that is not from love.

There is only love ... there is only the protection of Divine Source and that of my brethren and me.

If you cannot release all that you desire into the Light of Divine Source ... how shall you then communicate with you, discovering that which you truly desire?

Release the fear of not manifesting all that you desire.

Open your heart and mind to receiving all that is already yours in the Realm of Spirit. Open your heart and mind to receiving all that is being made manifest in the physical realm.

Declare your intentions with clarity from the heart.

You know that which you most desire. Are you then going to choose to deny you that which is already yours?

Day 32

GO WITHIN
Emmanuel

Seek the answer to all within you.
Seek the answer to all knowing the answer is made manifest simply for
the asking.
In the asking all is made known to you.
In the asking all is given you.
In the asking all is prepared for you.
There is nothing that cannot be transformed ... a silken worm spins a
cocoon going within, merging the old with the new, renewing itself in
the process.
In much the same way, going within, seeking answers to that which faces
you this moment, you transmute the old, merging the new, renewing
your Inner Spirit and those around you.
You need only ask for my assistance, light an orange candle.
Call my name. Speak from the heart. Know I am instantly by your side..
Know you are enfolded in unconditional love.
Feel your heart release all that is not of love. Release any perceived
shadow.
Release all that is not of light.
Know I hear your every whisper.
Know the way is made clear.
Beloved Child of Divine Source, what is it you seek?
Can you not see it is already so?
Go within; believe all is well. Believe all is well.

Day 33

LOVE THE SELF
Mihr

∽◈∽

For you to be loved, you must first love you.
For you to be loved, you must be loving to you and to others.
In the loving of you, you are projecting that which you desire most,
connection to another through love.
Do you not desire connection?
Do you not desire to express yourself freely?
Do you not desire to be loved freely without condition?
Is it possible to have one without the other?
We say it is not possible.
If such a being comes to you withholding even one hand from you, how
then can it be truth?
Do you wish to walk in the Light and Love of Divine Source and that of
my brethren? Offer first love and light to you, for it is in the giving there
is having the gift of love and light to share with others.
It is not possible to give to another that which you would withhold from
you.
Love you as you would love another.
Give to you as you would give to another.
Call upon me; I shall assist you in opening your heart to receive all that
you desire and more.
It is in the giving that you receive.

Day 34

YOUTHFUL SPIRIT
Guardian Angel of Youth

As you travel along the path before you, do you stop along the way
marveling at the many gifts before you?
Do you ponder only what has come before unaware of all that surrounds
you?
Do you delight in seemingly small things?
Do you delight in seeing beautiful flowers or hearing a song bird?
The tenderness of youth is within you.
What delights the child within?
Nurture the child within.
Stop along the journey before you.
Light a candle, play music, sit in the silence, listen to the breeze play in
the trees.
Close your eyes.
What do you see?
How shall you choose to honor the child within this day?

Day 35

AWAKENING YOUR INNER ESSENCE
Remiel

⌒⋔⌒

What does being awakened mean to you? Is it a feeling?
It is a sense of something wondrous?
Perhaps you are unsure what to be awakened really means?
If you are willing to travel in your mind to the Realm of Spirit, sit back,
breathe deeply .. hold this breath for a moment, exhaling any stress or
strain you may be feeling in your physical, emotional or mental body.
Breathe in .... breathe out.... breathe in .... breathe out ...
Feel your body free itself from any burdens.
Pause for a few moments. Calm your mind, slow your heart rate, focus
on your breathing ... what do you see? What do you feel or sense?
Do you perhaps sense peaceful bliss deep within your physical body?
See or feel this sense of peaceful bliss begin to expand within you as it
radiates outward filling your entire body, mind and soul with absolute
calm.
There is only peace. There is only harmony.
Your inner essence awakens as you travel the path before you.
In this place of peace and harmony, there is only joy. In this place of
peace and harmony, there is only Divine Love, freedom from all worldly
distractions.
You are always connected to that which is always within you.
Awakening your inner essence connects you more purely, more openly
with who you truly are, a beloved child of the Divine Source and to all
Angelic Beings in all Realms.

Day 36

BALANCE
Archangel Metatron

✒

There is balance in all things.
There is harmony in all things.
There is serenity with every breath.
If there is not balance, harmony or serenity within you, how then shall
you know your connection with Divine Source?
Hear me beloved child, there is much to celebrate for you are loved.
Do you not feel the wind brush across your skin?
Do you not smile at the sight of beauty on the land?
Take your hand holding it to the light ... is it not a wondrous joy to see
such perfection? In this perfection see you.
Each thought has the power to manifest in physical form.
What thoughts command your attention?
Thoughts direct your vibration.
Your vibration manifests unto itself like thoughts.
You are the keeper of your thoughts, of your vibration.
How shall you choose to this day?

HEART CENTER
Barakiel

~*~

You have seen many things in the physical realm and in that of Spirit.
What is it you truly seek?
Do you seek for the betterment of yourself for you and that of others?
It matters not what you seek or why you seek it.
The seeking must begin from the Heart center, your Heart center.
Speaking, thinking, acting from the Heart center deepens your
connection with Divine Source.
Do you wish to see differently?
Do you wish to create abundance?
Do you wish to lighten your present moments?
Light a deep purple candle; call my name softly three times.
Light incense which reminds you of the forest.
Focus upon your desires.
Fill your desires with truth, love, laughter and joy.
Know your prayers are answered in the moment of the asking.
Know that all is made manifest in the moment of the asking.
Be open to receiving that which you desire most, know it is so.

Day 38

WISDOM
Guardian Angel of Wisdom

⌒✻⌒

Wisdom manifests on so many levels, each level providing the
opportunity to choose that which you desire most.
The physical realm is a delight to the senses in all manner of form and
substance.
With each step along the path before you, distractions arise.
Choose the vibrational frequency you desire as you focus your thoughts,
actions or emotions.
How shall you choose this day?

Day 39

CLEAR COMMUNICATION
Bath Kol

⌒✕⌒

A fine mist of soft lavender light surrounds you.
Breathe in lavender light, breathe out distrust.
Breathe in lavender light, breathe out bitterness.
Breathe in lavender light, breathe out white light.
Breathe in lavender light, breathe out lavender light.
Feel your physical body sigh, releasing all that is not truth.
In loving yourself, you must speak the truth from within, that which
makes your Soul sing ... that which creates song within your entire
being.
Wrap you in lavender light; imagine lavender wings enfold you softly,
gently as if to caress you into a state grace.
Do you wish to know your truth?
Do you wish to know your life's purpose?
Do you wish to deepen your love of Self as Divine Source intended?
Do you wish to speak with clarity, releasing you from all thoughts of
emotional bondage or denial?
Open your to heart to all that is, accept that which you desire most for it
is already given you.
Open your heart, sing my name three times, light a lavender candle.
Know I am with you by your side lovingly guiding you to all that awaits
you.

Day 40

RISE ABOVE
Angel of Discernment

⌒*ᴍ*⌒

The physical realm presents many opportunities to rise above the
seeming chaos of everyday distractions.
Each distraction may be looked upon as a blessing or potential conflict.
Choosing to focus on the distraction itself or that which is beyond the
distraction is rising above.
As you travel the path before you knowing all that awaits, trust you are
exactly where you are meant to be in this moment.
There are many moments that have come before and many moments yet
to come. Where shall you choose to focus your light, your energy from
within?
There is only light and love from Divine Source. Honor yourself in
choosing to focus past that which appears before you, attempting to
distract you from your life's purpose ... away from the light even for a
moment.
Choose illumination.
Choose to rise above this day and all your days before you.

Day 41

PROTECTORS AMONG US
Archangel Gabriel

Moments of darkness appear where Light and Love seek to illuminate
the way before us all.
Turn your thoughts to those who are far from their homes.
Turn your thoughts to all who have transitioned from the earthly realm
to that of Spirit. Turn your thoughts to all who seek to protect you from
another's harm be it thought or physical, mental or emotional harm.
Turn your thoughts in gratitude for all who have given their physical life
for you this day and all the days that have come before.
Turn your thoughts to all who gave of themselves without thought or
delay.
Turn your thoughts to all whose blood has shed to protect you.
Turn your thoughts to all who are not free in mind, body, heart or
Spirit.
Turn your thoughts to all who pass your way this day.
Turn your thoughts to the protectors among us, my brethren and me for
we are always by your side.

Day 42

CREATIVE VISUALIZATION
Samandiriel

⌐₥⌐

Open your mind. Open your heart. Open your ears. Open your Spirit,
hear the calling within you.
What is it you most desire for your life in the physical realm?
In creating one's reality, give your thoughts, emotions, your Spirit the
gift of flight. Flight is a most precious gift of freedom, the freedom to
soar beyond all limitations, real or perceived.
Dare to dream, dare to change the reality in which you find yourself in
this moment. This too shall pass...as you shall not pass this way again.
Create the way before you.
As you create an alternative reality and focus upon it, it becomes your
reality.
For in the creating there is truth.
See your truth differently and the truth you see will be different.
Open your mind. Open your heart. Open your ears. Open your Spirit,
hear the calling within you.
What will you dare to dream this day?

Day 43

SPIRIT OF FAITH
Djibil

⌒✿⌒

In the days ahead, know all is in Divine Order according to the Divine
Plan for your Life's Purpose.
There is nothing one needs to learn, or do or have to attain oneness with
Divine Source. Simply open yourself with grace and ease to all that is,
accepting unconditional love and light, knowing all is given for the
asking
All is answered in the seeking.
Knock and the door shall be opened to you. I, Djibil, Angel of Faithful
Spirit is always by your side, guiding your thoughts, guiding your heart
center to that place of knowing all is indeed well with you.
Reach within, touching that place where faith and love are limitless,
unconditional gifts freely given you by Divine Source.
Go forth this day knowing all is well with you beloved Child.

Day 44

DIVINE GUIDANCE
Angel of Divine Guidance

≈

There is no limit to the ways in which Divine Guidance is given.
The song on the radio ... a soft breeze across your face ... a friend who
reaches out to you at just the right moment ... a soft whisper from just
behind your ears.
Divine Guidance is for the asking.
What is before you this moment for which you are wanting clarity or a
peaceful resolution?
What is your inner most desire?
Do you ask Angels, Divine Source or your Guides for guidance?
How does one request Divine Guidance?
Breathe in light exhale shadow or darkness.
Be clear in your asking.
Be open to receiving.
Divine Guidance is yours for the asking.
Divine Guidance is yours for the seeking.
Divine Guidance is yours for the receiving.
What do you ask this day?
What do you seek this day?
Are you open to receiving that which you have asked and that which
you seek?

Day 45

OPEN YOUR HEART
Muriel

⌒*⌒*

Open first your heart to yourself. Love you without reservation.
In what ways do you express love for yourself and others?
What service or services do you render simply for the joy of doing so?
An open heart expresses love easily, without reservation or judgment.
An open heart radiates peace, joy and harmony to all who would see the
gift before them.
Dear Child of Divine Source, how do you choose to travel the path
along the journey before you?
Do you choose to close your Heart from all that is before you?
Do you choose to willingly open your heart to all who grace your path?
Choose wisely child of Divine Source, for in the choosing so lay the path
before you. Travel this day in peace and harmony.

Day 46

MUSIC WITHIN
Israfel

⌒⁓

Listen to the beating of your heart.
Listen to the sound of your Soul.
Chanting resonates your entire being with the Divine Source.
Chanting, singing, humming ... all resonate deep within you core, re-
connecting, re-aligning you with your true essence.
Travel the physical realm in joy and harmony.
Experience joy, all else flows gracefully as you glide along the path before
you.
Do you desire to burn-off limiting thoughts, releasing that which
attempts to restrict your inner essence from shinning forth?
Divine Source sees only your true essence.
How then can a thought, a feeling, an action past, given you by your
physical self or another, possibly inhibit that which is eternal, that which
is from the Light of Divine Source
Sing out this day; chant "OM" till it resonates within your entire being
physical and ethereal.
Sing out this day.

Day 47

BREATHE
Guardian Angel of Harmony

The day brings forth many opportunities to focus, perhaps even re-focus our thoughts, emotions and actions.
Remember to breathe.
Breathe deeply ... hold your breath for a moment.
Exhale slowly.
The pace of the day, of the season will at first appear to gain momentum.
You can choose to step aside, allowing harmony and peace to be your guide this day.

Day 48

DIVINE GRACE
Kabshiel

Glide through the moments before you with the ease of a bird in flight.
Imagine floating through the air as a beautiful Butterfly, dancing in the breeze.
Allow all your cares and worries, perceived or real, to simply float away from your thoughts in a soft rose colored bubble.
That which is before you this moment, see through the eyes of compassion, see through the eyes of love, see through the eyes of forgiveness.
Grace asks you to dance with her, feel your heart and Soul release all that is not of love, all that is not of light.
Radiate peace and joy.
Radiate harmony.
Radiate love and light.
Radiate compassion for you and those around you.
Dance with grace this day.

Day 49

ONENESS
Omniel

⌒✻⌒

The concept of Oneness may at times feel elusive.
If we, in physical form are always connected to Divine Source, then why
do we at times feel as though we are alone?
The ego voice fears non-existence.
As you become more closely aligned with Divine Source, the ego voice
will attempt to distract you from your journey of peace, harmony and
joy.
The feeling of separation manifests in all manner or form.
Perhaps you are experiencing lack along the journey ... lack of love, lack
of abundance, lack of health, lack of peace.
It is in the feeling or sensing lack, that the true essence of oneness eludes
each one of us. In truth, there is only the perception of lack.
There is only the perception of separateness from the one Source of All
There Is. Acknowledge that which appears before you this moment.
There is nothing that cannot be healed with love and light.
Seek that which feeds your very heart and soul.
Focus on that which brings you joy.
Focus your thoughts, your emotions, your actions to that which you
desire most.
Re-focus whenever a thought or feeling attempts to distract you from
where you choose to be.
Reach out to another, release all that is not of your choosing.
There is nothing to great or too small for Divine Source.
Sit in the silence, remember who you are.

Day 50

MINDFULNESS
Guardian Angel of Mindfulness

Be present in this moment.
Allow your mind, your emotions, your actions to reflect upon all that
brings you to the moment before you.
How shall you choose to align you with Divine Source?
How shall you choose to open yourself, re-connecting with Divine
Source?
Gratitude, patience, compassion, all is seen through the eyes of
Unconditional Love.
What do you see?
Looking past earthly realm perceptions and appearances ... what do you
truly see? Beloved Child of the Universe, you are light and love, you are
perfect health, you are prosperous beyond measure.
Look again, what do you see?
Be kind to you, nurture your true Soul essence.
Direct your thoughts to all things positive.
Each experience is a gift.
Yes, even experiences which appear to be less than kind and loving.
You have a choice. Choose wisely for in the choosing to see, feel or speak
differently, lay the true gift.
Change the way you see things and the things you see change.
Be mindful of where you are.
Be mindful of where you choose to be. Be mindful of choices made.
Be mindful of your inner essence.

Day 51

STILLNESS
Guardian Angel of Stillness

Be in the moment. Be in the silence.
Quiet your mind, deepen your breath.
Allow your physical body to release all it is carrying within and around it.
Feel the tension in your shoulders and neck simply melt from you.
Be in the silence.
What do you hear outside of yourself?
Listen with your physical ears. Listen with your inner ears.
Breathe deeply and slowly, pausing as you fill your entire Being with the love and light of Divine Source.
Be in the gap; be in the moment, feel or sense the stillness in between thoughts.
Be in the silence.
Allow you the gift of silence.
Do you not feel a sense of peace?
Delight in the gift of stillness ... for in stillness all things are possible.

Day 52

EMPOWERMENT
Jeduthun

Finding the spark of truth within is a most powerful gift of
empowerment.
Rub your hands together. Gently place your hands about your throat.
As you close your eyes sense love caressing your inner voice.
What truth do you wish to speak?
What truth have you been holding from yourself? What truth do you
seek?
Surround you Self with soft aquamarine light. Light an aquamarine or
white candle. Focus your gaze on the flame of the candle clearing your
mind of all things.
Imagine a sweet soothing voice. This is the sweet melodic voice of Angel
Jeduthun.
Do you seek inner strength in speaking your truth to you and others?
Do you wish to release negative thoughts about anything or anyone?
Perhaps you seek empowerment from within the center of your physical
body?
Imagine what it would feel like, sound like.
How does empowerment transform that which is before you this
moment?
Breathe deeply, infuse this feeling, this knowing within you.
Allow all you sense, to bring a smile to your beautiful Angelic face.
Feel the smile float all around your physical body, feel the smile radiate
from within to all around you.
Feel your entire being sigh in love, light and harmony.
Give the gift of your smile.
Give the gift of empowerment to you this day.

Day 53

LIMITING BELIEFS
Ohrmazd

⁓✐⁓

Release all that no longer serves you.
Release all negative thoughts, all negative emotions.
Negativity will only serve to hold from you that which you most desire.
See through the eyes of love.
Limiting beliefs, limiting behaviors seek only to limit you and all you
desire.
Limiting thoughts, emotions, and beliefs seek only the lowest of
vibrations.
Release all that is not borne of love.
Allow your Spirit to soar among the clouds.
See and feel with an inner knowing that all is before you this moment.
How shall you choose to be the bearer of peace, hope and wisdom this
day?

Day 54

STRENGTH
Guardian Angel of Strength

Strength manifests itself in many ways.
The gift of discernment is knowing when to speak your truth and when to keep your truth close to your heart.
Gift of Light ... the path before you may present opportunities to dim the Light within you.
Instead choose to shine, radiating light and love.
Gift of hearing ... as you grace the path before you, give the gift of hearing you.
Give the gift of hearing those around you. There are many among us who crave to be heard. Give the gift of listening.
Gift of Joy ... give your smile to another today. Speak words of kindness to you and those around you.
There are many attempts to distract you from your path.
Allow you to acknowledge the distractions for what they are, perceived detours.
The main path is before you, gift you with loving kindness.
Grace your Spirit with love and light, always moving forward.
There are countless ways in which you express strength each and every step along the journey.
Rejoice, for you continue to place one foot in front of the other.
Rejoice for you shine for all to see. Rejoice for in giving so shall you receive.
See a beautiful bubble of bright white light all around your physical body.
See or feel the bubble of bright white light extend in all directions

around you.

The bubble enfolds you in soft, gentle, loving energy. The bubble of beautiful white light gently wraps itself around your physical body; extending 3 feet in front, back, above and below.

Imagine a soft cocoon of loving white light all around you, allowing only that which is borne of love and light to join with your energy.

Travel the path before you, love and light are you strength.

Day 55

INNER BEAUTY
Guardian Angel of Divinity

The Spark of Divinity is within each and every living creature.
Light a candle, breathe deeply, focus your mind as you inhale ... pause
for a moment ... exhale slowly.
As you breathe deeply feel or sense that place within you where you
experience joy, harmony and peace.
Gazing at the candle flame, focusing your thoughts and your emotions,
see or sense the inner Spark of Divinity within you.
The Spark of Divinity is the mirror of your own inner beauty, your true
essence.
That which you see in physical form is a reflection of your true essence.
It is said, "Beauty is in the eye of the beholder" ... behold you beloved
Child of Divine Source.
Release you from the bondage of others thoughts, emotions and the
actions of others. Allow all that is borne of love and light to shine forth
within and around you this day.

Day 56

DIVINE ORDER
Archangel Raguel

All is in Divine Order beloved child.
Rejoice in knowing that all is in Divine Order for it cannot be otherwise.
All things, people, places, and experiences are as they are to be this moment.
That is before you is a gift sowing itself in form or another. We hear your asking to understand.
Know and trust understanding is not always for your highest and best good.
Accept the gifts before you.
If the gift is not to your liking, surround it with loving rose light.
See the gift in the palm of your hand, allow the gift to float from you thus creating space for that which you truly desire.
Take a moment to truly see all that is before you, all that is behind you, and all that is yet to come.
Do you see through eyes of confusion or doubt?
Choose to see through eyes of love, trust, and those of faith.
Know Divine Source will have only good for all your days.
Know Divine Source sees only perfection.
See you through the eyes of Divine Source.
Choose to see past shadow and darkness.
Choose to see past doubt. Know all is in Divine Order this day...choosing to see beauty. Choose to see love and light.
All is in Divine Order this day.

Day 57

ANTICIPATION
Guardian Angel of Hope and Desire

Each day you wake to all that is before you.
Each day you wake to the gift of hope and desire. Each day you wake to the gift of choice.
Each day you wake with the gift of anticipation. What do you anticipate this day?
Do you anticipate harmony and peace all about you?
Or perhaps you anticipate shadow and darkness lurking about each turn.
As the sun rises each morn, the sky is painted with brilliant colors of soft rose, lilac, and sometimes iridescent orange-gold.
Does the sun tire of shinning forth each day?
Does the sun brood because its light appears to be hidden from view?
How then can you not choose to shine forth each moment as if for the first time?
Does the light of the sun cease in anticipation of clouds or the darkness of night?
Choice is the greatest of all gifts, for in choosing, anticipation and desire shine forth as a beacon for all to see. Desire to shine for you this day.
Beloved child, smooth your brow, open your eyes, choose to face that which is before you with love and light.
Gift yourself this day with compassion, hope, and with desire.

Day 58

BELIEVE
Guardian Angel of Belief

⚊ⁿ⚊

In what so ever you shall believe, it shall come to pass.
This we say to you, know all is before you.
Know all is given for the asking.
Know all is made known to you for the seeking.
Know all is opened to you for the knocking. All you desire is already
before you.
All you desire is made known to us.
All you ask, all you desire, all you seek is already given you.
Trust.
Believe.
Cast away doubt and fear.
Cast out all that is not borne of love this day. Open thy Self, open your
heart.
Accept gifts given you.
Trust.
Believe.
Have faith beloved child of Divine Source.
There is nothing too great or too small for the asking.
There is nothing too great or too small for the seeking.
There is nothing too great or too small for the giving.
Trust.
Believe.
Know all is in Divine Order this moment and the next.

Day 59

GUIDING LIGHT OF FAITH
Angel of Faith

⌒ᴎ⌒

All the days before you are illuminated with the light of Divine Source.
Have faith beloved child, for light and love shine forth from within you.
Cast out all that is not of love and light. Shadow and darkness are merely
distractions which lay in wait, tempting the ego to look away from the
light.
Look to the light, connect with Angels. All is well. All is in Divine
Order this day.
Be willing to see past shadow or doubt
Seek the path before you with anticipation and excitement.
Know all is answered in the asking.
Know you are protected, loved, and supported throughout all your days.
Surrender the outcome of all that lay before you...allow the Angel of
Faith to show you the way.
Have faith, the gift before you may be the answer to your quest.
The gift before you may be an assurance all is well. The gift before you
may help you choose more clearly.
There are no mistakes, there are no accidents...things, people,
experiences co-incide one with the other creating opportunities for
expansion.
Acknowledge the ego voice. Accept the gift with an open heart seeing all
possibilities ... choose with an open heart and open mind.
Faith is knowing the path before you is always illuminated with light.
Cast your fears, doubts and worries into the light.
Love and light shall prevail for all else is illusion.
Faith is knowing all is well, all is in Divine Order.

Day 60

COMPASSION
Angel of Compassion

Be compassionate with you this day. There is much ahead of you ...
know all is in Divine Order within and around you.
Judge not what is before you, observe, acknowledge, moving forward
one step at a time. Being compassionate is to be kind with you.
Being compassionate is offering non-resistance to experiences ... to the
actions of others. No, beloved child, we are not saying you must accept
that which is not of love.
We ask you consider offering non-resistance to that which is before you.
In offering non-resistance, negativity ceases.
Be kind to you this day.
Judge not your actions, thoughts, or emotions.
Judge not the thoughts, actions or emotions of those around you.
Compassion is understanding yourself, knowing there is so much more
than what appearances reveal to the naked eye.
Compassion is loving you as no other.
Compassion is sharing a smile, a kind word, giving of time to you and to
others. How shall you choose to express compassion this day?

TREE OF LIFE
Archangel Jophiel

Tree of Life ... when you hear or see these words what images grace your
inner sight? Imagine for a moment standing in the center of a lush,
beautiful forest.
Listen, for in the stillness there are many sounds of life, birds, the breeze
as it plays its sweet melody through the leaves.
Perhaps there is a stream or a waterfall nearby.
Breathe in the sweet scent of the forest.
Close your eyes.
What do you sense?
What do you see?
What do you hear?
Still your mind, still your heart, calm your emotions ... quiet the ego
voice within.
Breathe in golden yellow light ... exhale shadow and darkness.
Breathe in golden yellow light, feel or sense it infilling your entire being
radiating outward creating a beautiful bubble, enfolding you in
unconditional love and light.
Feel the warmth of the golden yellow bubble as it gently and lovingly
brushes your skin.
It may feel like silk or perhaps like butterfly wings.
Allow peace and harmony shall follow you all your days.

Day 62

ASK
Akatriel

⌒*∿*⌒

Ask and it shall be answered unto you.
Ask and ye shall receive.
Ask and it shall be revealed to you.
Ask and ye shall be healed.
As you ask for guidance, abundance, health, forgiveness, healing, or
protection, be willing to receive the answers you seek.
See with open eyes, signs are freely and easily given.
Hear with open ears, answers may be given in passing conversations or
song.
Ask from your heart center, set the intention to accept that which is
already yours. Listen with an open heart, an open mind, and open ears.
Accept that which is given.
Guidance from on high is positive and uplifting ... that which is borne
of love and light is for your highest and best good.
Shadow or darkness have no cause to enter your body temple, thoughts
or emotions. Goodness and mercy shall follow you all your days.
Walk upon the path before you with confidence, peace, joy, compassion
and in harmony. Go forth this day knowing all is in Divine Order and
occurring in Divine Time.

Day 63

STATE OF GRACE
Ananchel

Step into the light beloved child; tilt your loving face towards the
heavens.
Feel the warmth of the sun upon your face ... open your arms, open your
heart, open you to all that is.
Breathe deeply allowing your mind to become still ... in the silence one
hears many things.
Listen, listen, listen ... all you seek is already within you.
Grace is knowing all is well, all is peaceful. A state of grace is manifested
in many ways ... a smile shared by two, contentment, an unexpected gift.
Look about yourself this day. Ananchel, the Angel of Grace is you.
Do you choose to see with an open heart?
Do you choose to experience grace this day?
Grace is that place or space within you and around you, allowing you to
simply be.
Just for a moment, close your eyes ... see that which is within. The light
within you is strong, bright, a beacon for all to see. See you dear one, for
you are a gift to all who would see the light.
As you travel the path before you this day, allow kindness and mercy to
be your companions.

Day 64

DAWN BREAKS THROUGH THE DARKNESS OF NIGHT

Angel of Dawn

⌒⁄⁄⌒

With the rising of the sun, a new day begins ... choices abound for you.
The unknown is not to be feared.
The unknown is to be celebrated, for in not knowing the outcome the magic unfolds before you.
Release the outcome of that which is before you.
Release the attachment to that which you seek.
In the seeking, there is joy.
In the asking, there is knowledge.
In the knocking, all is revealed.
Dawn breaks through the darkness of night ... light shines through perceived darkness. Illuminate that which you strive to surrender.
It is in the light, all is revealed, all is made known to you.
Seek first the light, all else is illusion.
Seek first the light and love of Divine Source.
Release you from self-judgment and from the judgments of others.
Release fear.
Release worry.
Release all that is not borne of love.
Surrender all that you are into the light and love of Divine Source.
All is given you this day and the next.
Rejoice for in the releasing, you become free to soar as it is intended.

Day 65

TRANQUILITY
Valoel

⌒✿⌒

In the dawning of new experiences, allow you to be enfolded in total
peace and contentment.
Wings of serenity gently, lovingly wrap around your entire being,
physical and ethereal. Breathe deeply, feel or sense peace and tranquility
flow through your heart and your mind.
Imagine ... imagine floating in a beautiful lake. You are safe and
protected as you open yourself to total, peaceful bliss.
The gentle, calm lake is the most beautiful aquamarine.
Clouds float effortlessly in the sky above.
Quiet your mind; listen to the soft sounds of the breeze in the trees
along the shoreline.
The clouds appear so close you could reach out and touch the
translucent iridescent white puffs.
Peace and serenity flow in and around you
There is only peace and serenity.
Are you smiling with ease this day, as peace and serenity envelope you in
its loving cocoon?
Tranquility is the gift of allowing, allowing all to be in perfect harmony.

Day 66

LIFE REVIEW
Archangel Jeremiel

Now is the time to observe that which is behind you, all that has come
before, bringing you to this moment.
Do not dwell, it is enough to acknowledge what was.
Know all is in Divine Order, all is forgiven this day.
You have the choice to move forward toward your good, that which is
for your highest and best good.
How shall you choose to travel the path before you?
Do you choose to experience joy, happiness, contentment?
Ponder for a moment that which has brought to this moment ... would
you choose differently?
Re-create the image or experience differently; allowing you to forgive
what was, knowing all is well; all is as it should be.
See through the eyes of discernment.
See through the eyes of love.
See through the eyes of compassion, compassion for yourself and for
others as you travel the path before you.
Allow the mercy of Divine Source and that of Angels to bathe you in
love and light, for there is only love and light.
Shed what was, much like the butterfly emerging from its cocoon,
transforming what was before, to what is.
Seek that which you know to be your truth, shine forth this day and the
next.
You are loved beyond measure beloved child.

Day 67

YOU ARE NOT ALONE
Archangel Taharial

⤳

Beloved Child, as you travel the earthly realm know you are loved, cherished, and protected. Yes, we understand you may at times feel as though you are alone.

During moments of perceived alone-ness, know there are multitudes of celestial beings awaiting to be beckoned to your side.

A whispered prayer, a thought, a longing to be in a better place ... that is all that is needed to summon us to your side.

Truth be told, we are always about you, shielding, guiding, loving, healing ... reminding you of your inner essence, your Divine Nature, that which is like unto Divine Source.

That which is your inner essence is pure, whole, it is complete as it is intended.

Seek first that place within, knowing love and light follow you all of your days.

Know love and light guide you all of your days. Know love and light shine forth from within you and through you. You are the light of Divine Source.

You are the heart of Divine Source.

How then shall there be anything less than love and light within and without?

It can not be otherwise, for there is only love and light, all else is illusion, perceptions not of your making.

Choose wisely, for in choosing, you choose light, or shadow and darkness.

Illuminate all with the love and light of the Divine, there can only be that which is pure in thought, pure in heart, pure in deed.

Call upon me to purify the mind, the heart, the Spirit ... the essence of your Soul.

Know all is well dear Child, for the dawning of the day brings hope, faith, trust and all is well. So be it. So be it. So be it.

Go forth, radiating light from within, become a softer, stronger beacon of the Divine.

Day 68

LIGHT WITHIN
Archangel Michael

⤳

In the dawning of a new day, hope, faith, and trust are renewed,
delivering the unconditional promise of Divine Source's eternal light
and love.

There are many who would attempt to distract you from your life's
purpose, from speaking your truth or attempt to dissuade you from
seeking your heart's desires.

Close your eyes … breathe deeply filling your entire being … exhale
shadow or darkness. Breathe in light, exhale shadow. Breathe in light,
exhale light.

Imagine Archangel Michael standing before you … a pillar of strength
and of righteousness.

Imagine, with your inner sight, Archangel Michael standing before you,
holding his sword in his hands, the tip of the sword gently touching
Mother Earth. His great sword cuts through all negativity, severing all
negative attachments, clearing the path before you bathed in light … all
negativity in and around you is now released into the light for healing
and transmutation. No request is to great or too small.

See or sense the bright white light seeking your heart center, gently
reaching your inner core essence. As you continue to breathe in deeply,
exhaling slowly, the white light begins to expand within, illuminating
your entire physical and ethereal being.

There is no shadow or darkness for there is only light in all directions.
The spark of divinity within radiates outward.

In the light, there is no fear. In the light there is only love. Forgive you,
for in the light there is only love. Light a white candle; write your

thoughts upon paper....send your thoughts, your requests to Archangel Michael upon the flame of the candle. Know all is answered in the moment of the asking.

Know are loved beyond measure beloved child, for you are light and love.

Day 69

PRESENT MOMENT
Angel of the Presence and Inner Wisdom

Light a candle; see the Flame of Divinity reflected within you.
That which has come before brings you to this moment, to this place, to that which is before you now.
Bring all of your awareness to this moment, release all that has come before.
Seek not moments yet to be.
Rejoice for there shall not be another moment as precious as this moment.
Breathe in light, focus on the flame of the candle.
Do you sense warmth radiating within?
Look about you ... is there not much for which to be grateful this moment?
The gift of wisdom brings with it trust, faith, hope, anticipation, discernment, gratitude, and compassion.
Re-focus your thoughts, your emotions, aligning you with this moment.
There is only this moment, there is no other.
Yes, be aware and acknowledge that which must be attended to in the physical realm. Just for this moment, be in the moment. What so ever you focus upon, shall be, for it is law.
Rejoice, for this moment is unlike any other, it shall not pass this way again.
Carry the flame of Divinity within your heart center; it shall accompany you all your days.

Day 70

HONOR YOURSELF
Archangel Chamuel

There are those among you who would judge you.
Listen not to the words of others, for you are a beloved child of Divine
Source.
Dear one, to you we say ... love you, judge not the truth of who you are.
In loving you, you also love Divine Source.
In judging you or others, do you not condemn that which is to be
forgiven?
In forgiving, you release you from the bonds of limiting thoughts,
emotions, and perhaps actions that would only serve to dishonor you.
Turning the other cheek ... loving you, expressing love to others ... is
honoring you.
In honoring you, you honor Divine Source.
Do you seek a Spiritual path?
Perhaps you seek forgiveness for what has come before.
Or perhaps you seek a deeper understanding of your life's purpose.
It matters not what you seek, that you seek, is what matters.
Be receptive to that which you seek.
Open your mind, your heart, your ears.
If you desire to receive knowledge or guidance, be open to all that is
before you.
Be still; know all is in Divine Order.
Know all is occurring in Divine Time.
Honor this moment, acknowledge the moment that has come before
this one... be open to all the moments yet to be ...honor yourself.

Day 71

VISION
Angel of Vision

Vision is the gift of seeing, seeing that which you desire most with such fervor it becomes reality made manifest in physical form.
Vision is the gift of seeing beyond what is.
Vision is the gift of knowing all is all well, all is occurring in Divine Time and in Divine Order.
Vision is the gift of believing that which you desire to be your truth, your reality.
Vision is a gift of clarity, knowing the path before you is open no matter the distractions. Vision is seeing past that which no longer serves your highest and best good.
Vision is the gift of calm.
The gift of seeing, opens the way before you ... there are many signs, symbols, messages given thee through others.
Listen, for there is much to hear.
Open your heart for there is much to experience.
Open your mind for there is much to learn, much to know.
Vision is a gift.
How shall you choose to honor the precious gift of vision?

Day 72

NEW BEGINNINGS
Guardian Angel of New Beginnings

⌒*⌒

This is the day Divine Source hath made.
Does it appear a bit brighter, filled with a bit more promise?
How shall you greet this first day of the rest of your life?
What intentions will you choose to set for you?
How shall you choose to walk along the path opened before you?
Will you step forward with an open heart?
Perhaps you will choose to listen with your inner ears.
Embrace all the blessings in this moment for there is no other with
which to compare it. Beloved child of Divine Source ... all is before you,
all is within you, all is around you. Breathe deeply for there is much
before you, prepare yourself.
Surround yourself with those of like mind; embrace those who are
beginning their journey upon the Earthly realm for they are your
brethren in all ways.
Accept your true essence in love and through love.
There is only love and light, all else is illusion.
Fear not for the best is yet to be.

Day 73

GRATITUDE
Guardian Angel of Gratitude and Perception

That which is perceived can be achieved. That which is appreciated is
returned to you. Perception is a lens through which all is seen and
experienced. Fear or lack, are perceptions.
Love and harmony are perceptions. Which do you choose to focus your
thoughts upon?
Acknowledge where you are, look through the eyes of love, peace,
abundance, contentment and joy this day.
There is much to be grateful for, for without all the moments before this
moment you could not be where you are.
Take a few moments, review where you are, where you have been.
Where do you now choose to be?
Where do you choose to focus thy energy?
Do you wish to manifest more of the same?
Do you wish to manifest your heart's desires?
Begin this day appreciating all that you are, all that you have, all that you
do.
Give thanks for the many blessings seen and unseen along the path as
you journey in the Earthly realm.
Give thanks for all who share the journey with you.
The Realm of Spirit sees through the eyes of love, contentment,
abundance, peace, joy and harmony.
Express yourself in gratitude this day and every day.
You shall bring forth more love, joy, abundance, and harmony as you
travel the path before you.
Shall you choose to flow with grace and ease?

Shall you choose to accept all that you are in this moment, ever moving
towards all that you truly are?
How shall you choose to walk the path before you?

Day 74

INNER HARMONY
Archangel Metatron

Light a candle, focus upon the flame.
What do you see in the flame?
Look more closely, open your inner sight, seeing with your heart and Soul.
As you gaze at the flame of the candle, breathe deeply the light of Divine Source.
Exhale all fear and doubt. Breathe deeply from the light of the flame.
Know you are safe and protected, open your heart to your core essence
... exhale slowly, feel your entire being sigh in the release of all that is not of love, faith and harmony. Sense your entire being, physical and ethereal, in total harmony.
Stay in this moment, experience bliss, beloved child.
Know you are only a thought or heartbeat from this place.
Be kind to you as you journey the path before you.
Be compassionate with you and with those around you, for they are beginning to awaken in greater numbers.
Peace be with you this day and the next.

Day 75

DAWN OF A NEW AWARENESS
Angel of Reconciliation

Days gone by are remnants of what was.
Accepting all that has come before, opens the way for all that is.
All that is yet to be, is the dawning of a new awareness.
An awareness releasing all that no longer serves your highest and best good.
An awareness that possibilities are limitless, for there are no limits in the Realm of Spirit.
Limitation is an earthly realm perception.
Release past sorrows, hurts, disappointments.
Open you to forgiveness, love, mercy, compassion.
As you open your heart releasing what was, you begin to bring together all aspects of life, all aspects of desire.
Releasing what has come before opens the way before you, releasing your Spirit from the bondage of all that has come before.
Seize this moment full of life, love, wonder and awe of all that has befallen you, bringing you to this moment.
Is it not a revelation in itself, in all that has manifested, bringing you to this moment? All who share the journey with you have wondrous stories.
For all who journey seek the light.
Seek the light for it shall illuminate the path before you.
Seek the light, it shall accompany you all your days.

Day 76

REFLECTION OF YOUR INNER-SELF
Guardian Angel of the Soul

Dear beloved child, know you are so much more than the body in which
journey the Earthly realm, for there are so many whose awareness is only
with the outer, physical realm.
Be kind to you, be compassionate, be loving, for your very essence, your
Soul, is eternal light and love.
Each one of you is unique, therefore, the way or ways in which you
honor your Inner-Self is unique.
How shall you choose to honor the Spirit within you?
How shall you choose to release your Inner-Self from that which has
come before?
How shall you choose to honor the body in which you journey the
Earthly realm?
All begins with Self-love, compassion, forgiveness, kindness, radiating
light from within. The outer Self is a reflection of the Inner-Self.
To give from the heart is to receive in kind.
To be kind you must first be kind to you.
Choose to honor your Inner-Self with loving kindness, all else shall be in
harmony.

Day 77

PROTECTION OF THE SELF
Angel Yephiel

⌇

With each step along the journey before you, words, thoughts and deeds
of others attempt to distract, seeking to sever your connection with
Divine Source.
Connection with Divine Source can never be severed for it has no
beginning nor has no end.
Your connection to Divine Source of all there is, is infinity itself.
During perceived moments of dis-connection, call upon me wrapping
your physical body in my protective energy.
Imagine a beautiful, brilliant white light wrapped around your entire
being.
Now imagine the white light surrounded by rose light, which in turn is
surrounded by deep green tourmaline light.
The purity of white light, loving rose light and protective tourmaline
lights shines forth as a beacon before you, behind you, above you and
below your feet.
Know, all that is not of love, is deflected away from you.
Breathe in white light.
Fill your entire being with pure, cleansing white light.
Know you are safe now and always beloved child.
Call upon me and my brethren.
Go forth this day knowing you are always protected.

Day 78

BELIEF IN THE INFINITE
Sahaqiel

Turn your eyes upward, look into the heavens for there is no limitation.
Ponder if you will the color of the sky.
The colors are seamless flowing one into the other.
In the wee hours of the morn, do you gift you with time, seeing all there is to see?
Do you give pause seeing the light at the tops of mountains or tree tops?
Do you notice the colors of the morn as the sun rises to greet each day?
How then can you not believe in the infinite?
There is nothing to small or too great to contemplate.
There is nothing to small or too great to move through.
There is nothing to great or too small for you to manifest.
Your desires build one upon the other.
Yes, even those desires seemingly unfilled for in unfilled desires, new desires are given wings to fly.
Soar beloved child for there is only you which holds from all that you truly desire.
Soar free into the limitless sky above you, for in truth there is only that which is infinite.

Day 79

LIGHT FROM WITHIN
Angel of Illumination

Light shines from within, around and through you.
With each step, with each stopping along the way, light shines upon the
path before you.
Do not fear the brilliance which shines forth from within you.
Allow you to shine as the brightest star among the heavens.
You are a beacon for yourself and for others you meet along the way.
Be not afraid; ask not how the journey will unfold ... ask instead to
accept all that you are.

Day 80

CLARITY
Guardian Angel of Clarity

As you look into the eyes of those around you, what do you choose to
see?
Do you choose to see anger, hatred, or fear?
Do you choose to see past perceptions of the Earthly realm, into the
heart and Soul of another?
Each moment you take breathe, each moment you feel the beating of
your heart is an opportunity to choose.
We do not say you must deny that another has a different reality for
themselves.
We ask you open your mind, your thoughts to seeing past perceived
limited thoughts and beliefs of others, acknowledging each creature is
free to choose for themselves. Choosing for one's self is a choice.
We ask you choose only for yourself allowing another to choose for
themselves.
In choosing for another, you deny others the possibility of choosing
differently for themselves.
Seek clarity within you, all else shall come to you in grace and harmony.
Step lightly upon the path before you.

Day 81

VISION
Archangel Jeremiel

Whatever you shall envision with your inner sight, so shall it be in the
Earthly realm. Inner strength, inner wisdom, inner sight, all are
reflected in the physical all around you.
What do you truly desire to manifest?
Do you seek to discover and live your life's purpose?
Do you seek peace and harmony about you?
Do you seek abundance and prosperity?
All is given for the asking beloved child of Divine Source.
Choose to open your inner sight. Choose to open your heart. Choose
to open your thoughts. In opening, you willingly embrace all that is
already yours.
In opening yourself, allow all that you are to shine forth, illuminating all
before you. See, hear, and feel all with love.
For in loving you, all that is not of love and light simply fall from you.
Be kind to you as you travel the path before you.
There are many who would tempt you to follow the old ways, returning
to that which is now behind you.
Light a purple candle, invoke the power within, hold the vision for yourself.
Ask and you shall receive.
Ask, for I and my brethren are already by your side.
Be of service to you and to others.
Seek first the light within.
The light shall radiate outward illuminating all, for there is only light,
there is only love. Be well, be kind, be alert, be loving, speak from the
heart, listen to that which resides within.
How shall you choose to illuminate thy inner vision this day?

Day 82

HONORING THE CONNECTION FROM WITHIN
Angel of Inner Essence

⌒*ᴍ*⌒

This day as all other days, is a gift.
How shall you choose to honor the connection from within?
Do you seek answers to your life's purpose?
Do you seek loving ways in which to express yourself?
Do you seek forgiveness or you?
Perhaps there is something or someone before you providing an
opportunity to go beyond known reactions to what has come before.
That which is in thy heart, thoughts and emotions this moment is a gift
to choose differently.
As with all things, moving beyond what is known, what was, remains
one step at a time. Travel this day in harmony, in peace.
Honor you.
Be in a state of gratitude for what was for it has brought you to where
you are.
Begin this moment, choose differently, honor the connection from
within.

Day 83

WISDOM AND HARMONY
Angels of Wisdom and Harmony

Reaching inward, seeking insight from Divine Source brings a hush to
all ego-chitter chatter of self-doubt, illuminating all that appears to be in
the shadow of darkness or fear.
Seek not the cracks and crevices of doubt or fear for these create only
more fear based thoughts, emotions and actions.
We ask instead, you focus on all that is of the Light of Divine Source.
Allow the light to shine in every place within you, see or feel the light
shine forth from within you.
There is only light, there is only love, all else is illusion.
As you align with Divine Source, you create space for harmony and joy.
Harmony and joy heal wounds of what has come before, making way for
what is and what is before you this moment.
With each breath, with each footfall along the path before you, choose
light, love, wisdom and harmony.
In the reaching for these things, all else falls away from you allowing
freedom to be who you truly are, a beacon of light in the darkness.
Ignite the flame of wisdom and truth within you.
See all illuminated with harmony and joy.
Honor you; choose to see through eyes of love and grace.
Choose wisely, for in the choosing, you choose the way before you.

Day 84

PROMISE OF NEW BEGINNINGS
Gazardiel

✧

The rising of the sun brings forth the promise of new beginnings.
Rise early, face the east, see the sun rise in all its magnificence.
Feel the warmth of the sun touch your physical body.
Imagine the dawn's early light illuminating the path before you.
With each step along the path, all is filled with light.
There is no darkness for each step, each experience, each thought, each
emotion brings you closer to that which you desire most, to be loved.
You are loved beyond measure for there is no time, space, nor distance
which separates you from that which you truly are.
Go within, the essence of your soul is always the same, truth, beauty, joy,
peaceful bliss. There is much to traverse in the physical realm, there is
much to see, feel, taste, hear, and to touch.
Use all to enrich this earthly experience. Surround yourself with
oranges, deep yellows, pinks, and purples.
All is yours for the accepting.
Reach for color within your heart space.
Reach for the energy of orange to guide your way.
Reach for rose, loving you and all that is before you.
Renew your Spirit.
Renew your Inner-Spirit with the dawning of each morn.
Know the sun rises to light the way. It is a symbol of everlasting hope
and renewal.
All is well. Believe ... know this is so.
Carry with you a token of color, reminding you of all we have shared
with you this day.

Day 85

IN THE SEEKING YOU SHALL FIND
ALL YOU DESIRE
Angel Pathiel

The door to all that you desire awaits the turning of the of the knob.
In the seeking you shall find.
In the listening you shall hear.
In the giving you shall receive.
In the asking all will be answered.
Be open to all that lay before you.
Be open to possibilities, for in possibilities lay manifestation.
Envision all that you are, all that you receive and all that you give,
flowing easily and freely.
In the giving of you to you, all that is within you radiates outward.
Give with an open hand and an open heart.
Receive with an open heart and open hand.
Gift another with your smile, compassion, joy and laughter.
There is no greater joy than loving another as you would love you.
Surround you with yellow light, light a yellow candle.
Focus your thoughts, your intentions, your heart.
There is no greater gift than love and light.
Shine forth this day, illuminate the path before you.

Day 86

SURRENDER PERCEPTION
Zachareal

Surrender is to release fear or doubt.
Surrender is allowing light to shine through the perception of darkness.
Surrender is allowing you to be one with Divine Source.
You are loved; you are a light in the darkness of perception.
Begin where you are, allowing your Inner-Self to experience all that you feel in this moment.
Are you willing to release shadow, doubt or fear? What do you truly fear?
Sit in the silence, breathe deeply ... exhale slowly and deeply.
Feel your physical body sigh with relief, feel your shoulders release all they carry. Breathe in ... exhale slowly. Allow your entire Being to release all that is not of love and light. Breathe in ... exhale slowly.
Does Ego-chitter chatter fill your thoughts? Gently bring the conscious mind to gentleness, to peace.
Begin to feel or sense harmony flow into the physical body easily and freely.
Is there a thought, an experience, or an emotion you are willing to truly look at, experiencing the emotion of that which is before you?
Allow the Inner-Self to fully feel the emotion, breathe deeply into the emotion ... exhale slowly. Slowly, ever so slowly, feel or sense all negative emotion begin to dissolve. Breathe deeply, exhaling slowly until all simply melts from you.
Sit in the silence for a few moments, allowing your Inner-Self to simply be.
Surrender all perception for there is only love, love for yourself, love for others.

Day 87

CLEARING THE PATH BEFORE YOU
Guardian Angels of the Path Before You

⁓✳⁓

This day as in all days, seek balance. Seek to balance emotion, thought, action. Seek to balance the outer Self with the inner Self.

Yes, we hear you saying there is not enough time, there is not enough money, there is no one to share my life, there are no jobs, there are few opportunities.

Choose to think, feel and speak differently. Choose to stop telling the story of lack and imitation.

Begin this day with new thoughts, new emotions, new actions.

Begin the telling of a new story ... there is enough time for everything.

There is enough prosperity, abundance for all you desire. There is someone to share your life, there are many to lovingly share my life.

There are countless opportunities.

Be not afraid of what has come before. Be not afraid of what is. Be not afraid of what is yet to come.

The path before you is safe; you are protected from all lower, negative energies. Surround you wings of golden light. Breathe in the light, exhale all that would hold you where you have already been.

In the light there is only abundance and prosperity beyond measure.

In the light there is enough for all to share. In the light there is an abundance of all things, in all places. Do you give of yourself without thought of that which you will receive in return? Do you give from the heart? In the giving, are you truly open to all that is already yours?

In the giving, are you open to receiving that which is given to you in kind?

Begin this moment, open your heart, your ears, your mind to all that awaits you.

For in truth, the path before you is paved with golden light and butterflies.

Day 88

DIVINE LIFE PURPOSE
Micah

cyf

Some look about and wonder why? Others look about and wonder why not?
Still others look about and wonder if there is something more.
The something more is your life's purpose, the Divine Plan for your
being in this moment, in this time, in this body.
All is revealed with each step along the path before you.
Yes, we understand there are missteps or distractions along the way.
Seek the gift in what appears to be misdirection, negative actions,
emotions, thoughts, which would seemingly hold you from all that you
desire, all you seek to experience. Understand there is only you who
truly keeps you from your highest and best good.
It is you. How does one remove themselves, allowing forward
movement towards your highest and best good?
Sit with yourself, light candles of gold sit in the silence, ponder without
limitation all you that see for yourself and the life you desire to live.
From where you are this moment, what step or steps are you willing to take?
What can you do beginning where you are?
You can choose to change your thoughts.
You can choose to change how you feel about where you are.
Choose to see light where the perception of darkness lay.
Choose to express gratitude, for in being grateful more of the same is
given to you.
Choose to see light expressing gratitude for the light.
Accept what has come before, knowing there is more waiting for you
when you choose to surrender all obstacles.
See the dawning of the path before you ... the way is made clear. The
choosing is yours.

Day 89

BLESSINGS
Angel of Appreciation and Gratitude

⌒ℳ⌒

There is much to be thankful for.
Look about you, what or who in your life are you grateful for?
In what ways do you appreciate you?
In what ways do you appreciate that which has been made manifest?
In what ways do you appreciate all who share your life?
What experience or situation do you wish to transform?
Are you willing to see and feel differently?
Are you willing to begin appreciating all that is in your life now, this
moment?
We offer this to you ... each day for seven days do not complain.
Each day for seven days, look about you; be aware of all gifts given to
you.
Are you willing to give the gift of your smile to another? Are you willing
to gift you with a smile, a kind word?
Gifts may manifest in the form of a phone call, an unexpected email, a
kind word, a cup of coffee, an opportunity to be of service.
There is no greater gift than being of service to yourself to others.
Being of service is not servitude.
Being of Service is giving from your heart.
Being of service is gifting another with a smile, a kind word.
There are countless ways in which blessings are given to you.
Be kind to you. Be loving with you.
Expressing love from within radiates outward illuminating all before
you.
Kindness and mercy shall follow you all your days.

Day 90

INNER SIGHT
Elemiah

Begin the day with silence.
Know yourself above all else.
Know your inner-most desires.
Know all is given to you for the asking.
In the silence, breathe deeply, illuminating your Inner-Self.
Prepare yourself, for the journey inward is most revealing.
Journey into your Inner-Being, seek your innermost truth.
Seek that core essence of you.
Seek the light from within, for there is only light.
Seek not outside of yourself, for that which is sought outside of yourself
cannot be sustained but for a moment.
Know you are safe and protected as you journey within.
What do you seek? Are you prepared to receive that which is asked for?
In the asking, all is revealed. In the asking, all is given.
All that you seek is within you this moment.
The path before you begins within.
How shall you choose to journey the path before you this day?

Day 91

SENSE OF SELF
Archangel Metatron

~*M*~

Breathe deeply beloved child for you are whole and complete. You are
created in the likeness and image of the Divine. You are whole and
complete.
There is nothing you lack. There is nothing you need do, or have.
Lack is the perception of being without that which you desire.
All is within you. All is given to you for the asking.
Do you look about you and see what is not yet manifested?
Or do you look about you in gratitude for all blessings bestowed upon
you?
Do you give thanks for this moment of life, the gift of seeing, the gift of
hearing, the gift of touch?
Do you seek guidance in all you do?
Are you open to receiving the guidance you seek?
Do you seek without first giving to you and to others?
Do you ask and then close your eyes to all that surrounds you?
Do you extend the hand of love to those in need?
Your sense of Self, knowing you are whole and complete as you are this
moment is the greatest gift of all.
Giving to you and to others becomes an act of loving kindness.
Treat you with the same love, mercy and compassion you would freely
give others.
As you give first to you, giving of yourself to others does not deplete you.
Breathe deeply beloved child ... you are whole and complete.

Day 92

ARE YOU PREPARED TO RECEIVE
Suriel

⌒*⌒

Self-created limiting beliefs, like any other, is a process.
You did not arrive where you are in the blink of an eye.
You arrived where you are with each footfall upon the path that is now
behind you. What do you desire to experience?
Do you wish to experience more love?
Do you wish to experience increased abundance and prosperity?
Do you wish to experience more joy? Or perhaps you wish to
experience increased peace and harmony.
Ask and it shall be given to you. Have you prepared yourself to receive
that which you ask?
Are you prepared to give to you all that you ask of others?
Limitation is within Ego–chitter chatter, absorbing your precious
energy of light and love.
Imagine deep amethyst purple all about you. Breathe deeply, allowing
the calm amethyst light to illuminate your entire Being.
See or sense the amethyst light begin to flow out from your core essence,
radiating outward, infusing all things with gentleness, peace, and
harmony.
Allow you to be in the moment. Allow you to see, feel, and hear beyond
the perception of reality.
Allow you to openly accept all that awaits you.
Begin this moment believing, thinking, seeing, hearing, and feeling
differently.
Prepare to receive. Prepare yourself for all you desire, for it is already so.

Day 93

RAINBOWS OF BLESSINGS
Archangel Raziel

Look to the heavens above, below, in front and behind you.
Look to the sky.
Look to that which is within you.
Look about you, for the blessings are many.
Reach inward, reach through the veil of all that has come before.
Look about you for there are rainbows of light, rainbows of blessings,
rainbows of creatures great and small among you.
Look about for there is only light, love, abundance, prosperity, peace,
harmony, joy and thanksgiving.
Look about you beloved child, you are loved beyond measure.
Look about you this day, give thanks for the creation of all that is.

Day 94

LIFTING THE VEIL OF DARKNESS
Archangel Zadkiel

Memories of all that have come before are within you.
The perception of good or bad is within you. For in the light, there is only love.
With each step along the path before you, seemingly insignificant memories of what once was may float to the surface.
Light a candle, allow the flame to show you the way to peace, harmony and joy.
In seeking these things, all simply falls from you, healing your Inner-Spirit, healing your physical being.
Imagine a heavy, dark curtain keeping the light of day from your eyes.
With your inner sight, pull back the curtain allowing even the tiniest ray of light to shine into the inky darkness.
Look about you, where there was once darkness, now there is light.
Now, if you are willing, pull the curtain back a bit farther.
Does not the light begin to illuminate all?
Breathe in light, exhale shadow or darkness ... breathe in light, exhale all that no longer serves your highest and best good.
Walk in the light beloved child, in the light all is healed.
In the light there is love, warmth, abundance and prosperity, harmony, peace, and joy beyond measure.
The light beckons you ... step into the light with an open heart beloved child.

Day 95

PRACTICING FAITH
Angel of Faith

Patience is your guide through days which appear to be fraught with the unknown. What situation or experience is before you this moment?
Allow you to see the golden ray of light, choosing to see beyond physical appearances. How does one exercise faith in the face of adversity?
Do you wish to feel differently?
Do you choose to see beyond the physical realm of limitation, fear, or anger?
We do not suggest you turn a blind eye to that which is happening to those around you. We are suggesting you merely observe that which occurs.
In the observing, allow all to flow around you.
Choose to allow only that which is positive to enter into your thoughts, your emotions, and your actions.
Do you know all that is to be in the moments ahead?
Do you choose to trust that all is well?
Do you choose to trust that there will be something to step upon or you shall be taught to fly?
Faith is in knowing I and my brethren through Divine Source, have provided all.
In the providing there can only be love, light, harmony, prosperity, joy, health, peace. Look about you, what do you choose to see this day?
How do you choose to walk the path before you?
Celebrate you and all that you are, know all is at it should be.
Celebrate knowing all is in Divine Order this day.
Faith in the unknown is a treasured gift only you can give to you.

Day 96

TAKE FLIGHT
Rampel

Be like the breeze, gently playful among the trees with soft melody for the Soul.

Close your eyes imagine the breeze playing upon your skin.

Allow all thoughts to simply be lifted from you.

Allow all emotion to smooth, blending with your entire Being.

Allow your Spirit to float among the tree tops.

Look about you, do you not see differently than when your feet were anchored into the soil beneath the trees?

Do you not feel free to take flight?

Allow your Spirit to discover your heart's desires. Allow you a sense of renewed passion for all you desire.

Be willing to weather the storm of uncertainty.

Be willing to soar to new heights.

In the releasing of what was, you open the way for that which is before you.

Take flight dear one, for you are given wings to soar above all that would hold you from your highest and best good.

Be strong for in strength there is grace, mercy and compassion.

Be willing to endure the pitfalls of perception for they attempt to distract you from your path.

Open you to all you desire for it is already given to you in the Realm of Spirit.

Day 97

SEA OF TRANQUILITY
Angel of Tranquility

⌒⋙⌒

This moment is all there is.
All that has come before has brought you to where you are.
Where do you wish to be in moments yet to come?
Close your eyes beloved child, float in total surrender.
Arms outstretched, surrender all that does not please you.
Surrender all that causes fear and doubt.
Surrender all that has come before.
Surrender the need to control that which is outside of you.
Surrender the need to control the path before you.
Surrender is sweet bliss for in surrendering all that is not of love, that
which is love surrounds thee in a sea of tranquility.
How shall you choose to surrender this day?

Day 98

FLAMES OF PASSION AND DESIRE
Angel of Divine Timing

⌒⋈⌒

All is well beloved child, for there is peace and harmony, joy and
laughter, health and wellness, abundance and prosperity all about you.
Light the flame of passion and desire within you.
Sense the spark of Divinity deep within, allow the embers of your
deepest desires to come alive.
Take time to fan the flames with patience, love, kindness, compassion,
faith and gratitude.
All is well.
Know all is according to Divine Timing, for all is revealed to you for the
asking.
All is revealed in the seeking.
All is revealed, for there are no secrets kept from you.
Know all is well; all is given to you without hesitation ... without
exception.
Know it is so. Know this to be truth. Know this to be your truth.

Day 99

AWAKENING YOUR SENSES
Angel Prince of the South

⌒*⌒

Step into the light of Divine Source. Step into the light, out of the
shadow of perceived darkness and fear based thoughts.
Allow that which is within to shine forth, radiating the magnificence of
your core essence.
Breathe deeply all that is of light and love for you are perfect, whole and
complete. Begin this moment seeing, hearing, feeling, tasting, and
touching with an open heart, an open mind.
Open your heart and mind to experiencing pleasure, joy, bliss.
Allow Earthly realm pleasures to guide you to your true essence of love
and light.
Free your thoughts from Earthly realm limitations.
Limitation is that which is appears to hold you from all that you are.
Close your eyes, listen ... listen ... what do you hear?
Sit in the stillness; hear the many sounds that surround you.
Open your mind, your thoughts ... go within, hear your inner voice
clearly ... it may be but a whisper. Listen, for in the listening you will
know yourself more easily, more completely.
Now imagine reaching out to touch something ... close your eyes, feel
the sensations in the tips of your fingers.
Do you choose to taste that which you eat?
Are you tasting fully that which you feed your physical body for sustenance?
Do you give freely of yourself to you and to others?
As you open your eyes, what do you see about you?
Do you take time to see?
There are many gifts for your viewing pleasure.
How shall you choose to awaken this day?

Day 100

SELF-EMPOWERMENT
Archangel Sandalphon

⌒◆⌒

What do you seek beloved child?
How do you seek the desires of your heart, mind, and spirit?
Ask and it is given. Knock and the door shall be opened to you. Seek and you shall find.
How do you communicate with your Inner-Spirit? Do you sit in the silence?
Do you speak your desires aloud? Do you speak silently, keeping all Sacred deep within? Do you write your desires and burn them by the flame of the candle?
Do you seek answers? Perhaps you seek forgiveness, love, abundance, harmony, or joy. In all things know your prayers are answered in the asking.
Be open to receive that which you desire.
Be open to receiving guidance in the form of whispered thought, people, songs, passing conversations, experiences, or passages in a book.
Be open to receiving that which you seek.
Give to yourself as you would give to others.
Love you as you would love others.
Be open to receiving that which you seek.
All shall be made manifest, for in the Realm of Spirit all is already yours in the moment of the asking.
Know it is so. In the asking, in the receiving, in the giving ...you shall find all, the way is made open to the you.

Day 101

EXPANSION OF THE SELF
Suriel

⤳✳︎⤳

In the dawning of each day, the sun rises to shine golden yellow light upon all there is. All of creation prospers in the light of day, resting in the darkness of night.

Darkness need not be your enemy. Shadow provides an opportunity for growth, for expansion, exploring your deepest desires.

Discernment is among your greatest gifts, for in discerning what do you do not want; you discover what do you want.

In discovering that which you desire, limiting beliefs, behaviors, thoughts, and feelings must release you from all that has brought you to this moment.

In the reaching for that which feels better, that which is for your highest and best good, your Inner-Self expands beyond what was.

Each step along the path before you is a choice to expand or remain where you are. Imagine you are a tree who has been *sleeping* through the shadow of winter.

In the warmth, feel the sap, the life blood within, begin to flow outward, beginning to expand beyond the physical barrier of your skin.

Imagine the life force within begin to push forth new ideas, releasing all that no longer serves you. Imagine buds begin to manifest all along your branches.

In the warmth of the golden yellow light, buds begin to blossom, bearing fruit or leaves, protecting all who seek protection.

Beloved child you are much like a magnificent tree which has been sleeping during the shadow of winter.

Allow you to blossom in the warmth of light and love.

Create love in your life and love shall be your expression for life.
Create vision in your life and you shall see beyond limitation.
Create joy and harmony in your life and you shall expand beyond your
known horizons. The choice remains with you.

Day 102

CREATING REALITY
Archangel Raguel

⟶

Limitation is an Earthly realm concept.
The Realm of Spirit knows only love and light.
In love, all things are created.
In light all is illuminated in joy.
Seek the light and love of Divine Source.
All is given in the asking.
There is nothing denied you.
Ego-chitter chatter is all that separates you from all you desire.
Choose to feel joy.
Choose to see through eyes of love.
Choose light and all that lurks in the shadows simply dissolves into the light.
As you travel the path before you, do you not place one foot in front of the other?
How then shall you expect to reach completion with one leap?
Traveling the path before you is best traveled one step at a time.
In re-focusing your thoughts all else vibrates or resonates differently.
You need only move forward one step at a time.
Enjoy the process.
Trust the process.
Be in a state of gratitude.
Cherish all as it unfolds before you.
The journey is the process.
Choosing creates the process, which in turn creates your reality.
How shall you choose to create for your vision for your life this day?

Day 103

INSIGHT INTO YOU
Satarel

⁓

Insight begins with a knowing that all is well, all is in Divine Order occurring in Divine Time.
Insight is discernment, knowing which is for your highest and best good.
Insight is trusting that all is given in the asking.
Insight is inner sight, knowing, believing, and having faith that all is as it should be in this moment.
Insight is following your inner guidance, the whisper of guidance resonating deep within you.
Insight is feeling, sensing, hearing, and knowing the difference between the Ego-chitter chatter and the stillness from which your Higher-Self guides you in the physical realm. Dare to dream.
Dare to hear.
Dare to see.
Dare to feel.
Dare to speak your truth.
Dare to be different.
Walk the path before you with love, wisdom, grace, and ease, in harmony and joy.
Light a candle, focus upon the flame.
See the colors within the flame.
It is time beloved child for you are whole, complete and perfect now, this moment and all the moments before you.

Day 104

POWER OF SELF LOVE
Hadraniel

Awaken the power of love within you beloved child, for you are eternal love and light. Walk the path before you in light, knowing all is made manifest before you.

Your prayers are answered in the moment of the asking.

You are guided this day and every day in love and light.

Fear not for we are beside you every moment.

You need only call upon us, we know your every thought, your every desire.

There is no asking to great or too small.

There is no asking left unanswered.

Sit in the silence, listen, open your heart to my brethren and me.

Know you are protected.

Know you are loved.

Know you are love eternal.

Know you are a bright light, a beacon for all who desire to see the path before them. Know you are a messenger of Divine Source.

Awaken the power of love within you.

We shall accompany you all your days.

Walk this day in love and light knowing all is indeed well with you.

Day 105

BALANCING STRENGTH AND WISDOM
Archangel Haniel

By the light of the silvery moon, renew your Spirit.
Balance in all things creates harmony; a sense of peacefulness enfolds you.
Inhale the sweet night air, knowing all is in Divine Order, occurring in Divine Time. Strength, balanced with wisdom creates calm within your Inner-Self.
Wisdom balanced with strength creates a knowing that all is being made manifest for your highest and best good.
There are no other desires than for you to be who you truly are, a beloved child filled with grace light.
Seek first your Inner-Spirit.
Illuminate your Inner-Spirit with the light and love of Divine Source.
Balance in all things ensures peace of mind, peace of body, peace within.
Seek balance in all things with all situations.
Balance strength with inner wisdom.
Balance inner wisdom with your inner and outer strength.
Accept that which is being offered to you.
Light the way before you with non-judgment unconditional love, with strength and wisdom.
All shall be revealed to you.
That which you seek is created in harmony with all things.

Day 106

ASK
Archangel Taharial

Beloved child you need only ask and it is answered.
Seek first the silence within.
Open your eyes, your ears to signs given to you for the asking.
Be still, knowing all is given to you.
Shadow is that which attempts to pull you from your chosen path, your chosen beliefs, knowing that all is well, all is in Divine Order.
Fear based thoughts create more fear based thoughts.
Re-focus thy thoughts, your emotions to that which brings joy, peace, and a smile to your loving face.
Re-focus your thoughts, your emotions knowing the perceived struggle within is Ego-chitter chatter attempting to distract you from the path before you.
Yes, the path may appear to be fraught with unforeseen dangers ... lack, dis-harmony, dis-ease, loneliness, fear of the unknown.
The path before you is filled with love, light, peace, harmony, joy, abundance and prosperity, health.
Be willing to trust guidance received through those close to you.
Be willing to trust your inner knowing.
Be willing to step of the edge of everything you have ever known.
Be willing to step beyond what was into what is.
Be willing to be willing ...

Day 107

LIGHT AMONG THE
SHADOWS OF DARKNESS
Archangel Michael

Call upon me for protection, clearing away all lower negative energies
from all places, situations.
Call upon me for protection from lower negative energies projected
from those about you.
As a moth is drawn to the flame, so shall your light attract many moths.
Many seek to illuminate their own spirits along their journey.
Some seek to extinguish the light of the flame.
Call upon me and my brethren beloved child, for the light of the
Creator shall shine forth through all layers of darkness.
Release that which does not belong to you.
Release the fear of being alone.
Release the fear of being unloved.
Release the fear of not having all you desire.
Open your heart, mind, body and Spirit to the all that is before you.
As the light within becomes brighter, know you will begin to vanish in
the eyes of some, for they will not be able to see you.
As the light within becomes stronger in its softness, know some will
attempt to extinguish the light within you.
Your faith, trust, inner strength, your knowing will be tested.
Remain strong, vigilant, against the darkness of others. There are many
over the ages who have sought to destroy, to conquer, attempting to
extinguish the Divine Spark within each of you.
Call upon me and my brethren, we shall protect and shield you from all
that is not of love and light.

Call upon me, I carry the sword of light mighty enough to clear away darkness and shadow.
Call upon me and my brethren, we shall light the way before you for all your days.

Day 108

RAISE YOUR VOICE
Jeduthun

⚏

Sing the praises of the Creator.
Sing praises for your many blessings.
Sing your hearts desires.
Sing to the heavens speaking your truth, let your voice be heard.
Release that which no longer serves you.
Release all that does not please you.
Open your heart and mind to the gentleness of clarity.
In the silence of the moment, listen to your inner voice.
Still the ego mind chatter for it desires dominion over you.
Call upon me, the Angelic choir shall join voices with you.
Raise your voice in celebration for the way is made clear before you.
Raise your voice, allowing you to be heard.
Soften your tone; soften your volume; allow you to be silent in times of
strife.
Give not to those who seek to quiet you.
Give not to worry; worry is fear based.
Sing the praises of the Creator. Allow your Spirit to be uplifted.
Allow your light to shine forth.
There is no judgment based in love.
Allow your Spirit to soar upon the wings of butterflies and dragonflies.
Allow your Spirit to soar upon the wings of birds and unicorns.
Allow your Spirit to soar freely among the winged creatures great and
small.
Raise your voice in celebration for all is revealed to you in the gentleness
of clarity.

Day 109

FORGIVENESS
Balthial

⌒〜〜

Forgiveness is releasing you from wounds caused by you or caused by another against you. Forgiveness releases you from harmful thoughts towards you and others.

Holding resentful thoughts towards a situation or anyone who contributed to a situation harms only you.

Call upon the Realm of Angels to assist and guide your thoughts and emotions away from what is already behind you to where you wish to be.

Thoughts and emotions govern your very being in the Earthly realm.

The why, how or when of things is not always apparent.

Know you are safe, protected and loved always.

It serves you not to harbor resentment or ill will towards another for in the end it harms only you. Free your heart and mind from all that is not based in love or you will you be in bondage to another's lower vibration.

There is only love. There is only light. Seeing through eyes of love, healing your heart serves your highest and best good.

Free you from the bonds of bitterness, despair, guilt, or anger. All are fear based thoughts, not worthy of your attention.

Give rise to your own Spirit; gift you with forgiveness, freeing you from all that is not based in love and light.

See that which calls your attention; tend to all things with loving kindness.

See the truth, move through pain and hurt as lovingly as possible, allowing the light of love to make the way clear before you.

Day 110

RELATIONSHIP HARMONY
Archangel Ariel

Purify your heart, your thoughts. Purify your Spirit. Purify your body.
You know what do to and how to do it.
Call upon me to assist you in your quest to purge all that is not of love
and light from within and about you.
Release all thoughts that are not of love, compassion, harmony, and joy.
Releasing all that does not serve your highest and best good, creates an
opportunity to see, hear, feel and think differently.
Allow the light of Angels and that of Divine Source, to flow into you
without hesitation. Step into the light; open your heart and mind,
embracing your true essence.
Seek harmony and balance within, all else shall re-align harmoniously
with the Divine. Quiet strength shall accompany you along the path.
Perhaps you seek harmonious resolution with another?
Step into the light, gently, lovingly. Speak that which needs to be
spoken with a soft tongue, gentleness in your thoughts and love in your
heart.
Seek peacefulness and peacefulness shall open the way before you. Seek
alignment with Divine Source. You know the way and the light, step
away from perceived shadow and darkness seeing the beauty of all
around you.
If you desire harmony, be harmonious. If you desire joy, be joyful.
If you desire resolution, seek first resolution within.
Be in harmony with you this day.

Day 111

MERCIFUL COMPASSION
Archangel Jeremiel

✧

Through mercy, you shall be merciful.
Through forgiveness, you shall be forgiving.
Through loving you, you shall be loving.
What do you seek to manifest?
What are your innermost desires?
How do you look upon you?
Do you believe it can be so?
Do you have faith and trust that it is so?
Step into the light beloved child for all shall be yours for the asking,
believing it to be so. All that has come before has brought you to this
moment.
This moment is all there is, open your mind and heart to all that is.
In this moment declare your innermost desires; create for you all that
you desire.
In the creating, release all that has come before with loving kindness,
mercy and compassion.
Moment upon moment love you, be merciful, be compassionate
allowing self-judgment to flow past you.
Rejoice for there is much to celebrate!
Be merciful, harmony shall balance all before you, within you and
around you.

Day 112

SIMPLY BE
Omniel

⌒ℳ⌒

Oneness, harmony, alignment ... become one with you, creating harmony, being in alignment.
In all things be true to you. In all things be true to you.
There can be only oneness for you are not separate from that of Divine Source.
There is only harmony for dis-harmony is fear based ego perception of being all alone. *All alone* when seen differently is *all one*, *all one* with Source Energy.
Oneness is being in harmony with your emotional heart center.
The heart of the matter is that you are always one with Source, always in harmony, always in alignment.
Appearances, perceptions attempt to distract you from that which is your truth.
Seek first the Kingdom of Heaven within; all shall be given to you in the moment of the asking, the seeking, the knocking.
All is given to you every time without exception.
In the Realm of Spirit, all is made manifest, you choose to see or not to see. You choose to hear or not to hear. You choose to experience or not to experience.
Become one with your desires, become one with your Inner-Self.
If you want prosperity, feel prosperous.
If you want love, be love.
If you want peace, be peaceful.
If you want harmony, be harmonious.
Be that which you are in the eyes of Source.
Simply Be.

Day 113

SOAR ABOVE YOUR CARES AND WORRIES
Nisroc

⌐yℓ⌐

There is much which faces you. Each moment, day, and night unfold with great mystery before you. How shall you choose to express your Inner-Self, that which is of love and light? How shall you choose to walk upon the path before you?

Imagine you are on the back of a great bird, a bird with great strength and gentleness. Allow your Spirit to release all earthly worries and concerns as you soar on the back of a great Eagle. Breathe deeply, for there is only the joy of simply being upon the back of this great bird. There is nothing to fear dear one for there is much to celebrate, much to be thankful for. Embrace the freedom to be who you truly are. Embrace the light, embrace the magnificence of this great bird as it enfolds thee in its majestic wings with tenderness and strength.

Love is all there is. Truth is all there is.

Allow you the freedom to experience all that is before you.

Choose to listen to your inner guidance. Reality is that which you create from within. Begin within you this moment, know your truth, live your truth, speak your truth.

The truth shall set you free to be your authentic Self, created in love, radiating light for all to see.

Walk in the light beloved child. Fear cannot hold you in the darkness of lack. Fear cannot hold thee from your good. Fear cannot withhold that which you desire most. Walk in the light beloved child, for the light shall cast out darkness and shadow before you, behind you, above you and below you.

Walk in the light; allow your inner light to shine with grace and ease.

We are many who guide you, love you, and protect you.
Be not afraid, for the light of Angels shall go before you. Be not afraid,
for the love of Angels shall embrace your all your days.
Allow your Inner-Spirit the freedom to simply Be.

Day 114

LISTEN
Archangel Zadkiel

Listen to the whispers of your inner voice.
Listen to whispers on the wind.
Listen to whispers delivered on butterfly wings.
Inner guidance is soft, subtle, and as soft as a whisper.
Sit in the silence, seek guidance from within.
Know the voice which radiates light and love.
Inner guidance is given with harmony and balance.
Be at peace, express joy.
Listen.

Day 115

MANIFEST JOY, MANIFEST HAPPINESS
Archangel Jophiel

Breathe deeply the scent of Mother Earth, exhale slowly releasing all that
no longer serves your highest and best good.
Breathe deeply, exhale slowly.
Imagine yourself in a meadow or a garden surrounded by the beauty of
Mother Earth. Breathe deeply, there are many scents of nature, exhale
slowly.
Stopping to look about you, what do you see?
Allow your inner spirit to dance and sing with joy.
Allow your Inner-Self to release any fears or sorrow from days long since
past.
Do you desire joy and happiness?
Be joyful, express joy with each breath.
Joy brings peace, harmony and happiness.
Joy is the elixir of life. Joy brings joyfulness.
Being in a state of joy opens the way before you, healing all that has
come before.
How shall you manifest joy this day?

Day 116

THAT WHICH COINCIDES
Guardian Angel of Focused Intention

∼✳∼

There are many distractions along the path before you.
Look about you; acknowledge all that is a part of your life in this
moment.
Look about you; keep your sight upon that which you desire most.
Each step along the path before you has the potential to be of value.
There are no mistakes. There are no coincidences, only that which
coincides one with the other.
Where is it that yourself along your path? What do you see happening
for you? With whom do you see you?
Focus upon that which you desire. Focus upon the joy of having, being,
doing that which you desire.
Express gratitude for all you are blessed with this moment. Express joy
in the giving of you to you and to others.
Celebrate this moment for there is much to be thankful for.
Focused intention on that which is for your highest and best good is one
of many ways in healing.
That which is before you, is the manifestation of all that has come
before.
This we say to you ... if you wish things to change, change the things you
focus upon; making way for all you desire to manifest along your path.
All shall be made manifest more completely, more lovingly, with joy.
Begin to look about you seeing all that which flows one into the other.
Be aware of where you are in this moment. Be aware of where you want
to be. Be aware of where you focus your energy.
Be aware of all about you, giving thanks for all that has come before
making way for all that is yet to be.

Day 117

WHISPERS ON THE WIND
Archangel Sandalphon

On the tips of Hummingbird wings, the soft beating of butterfly wings,
the silence of a feather in flight.
In the asking you receive.
In the wanting all is made manifest.
If you want love, be loving to you and to those around you.
If you want prosperity, be generous with you and to others.
If you want peace, be peaceful.
Be that which you seek and that which you seek shall be made manifest
before you.
You cannot receive that which you cannot give.
You cannot be that which you are not.
Be in the silence, look about you.
You are blessed beyond measure.
You are loved beyond measure.
You are prosperous beyond measure.
Go first within, all else shall be made manifest on the whispers of the
wind.
Listen, be open, give of yourself from your heart and soul.
Look first within, all shall be made manifest on the whispers of the
wind.

Day 118

INFINITE POSSIBILITIES
Archangel Raguel

Spring, a time of re-birth and renewal. Mother Earth begins to bloom,
springing forth after many months of seeming hibernation.
As you travel the path before you, do you not at times feel as though you
wake from a deep sleep?
Imagine waking from a very deep, very long sleep.
As you begin to open your eyes, what might be among the first things
you see?
Perhaps how blue the sky, how green the grass beneath your feet?
Are there clouds floating above?
Listen to the many sounds ... birds, a babbling creek nearby, perhaps
there is a slight breeze playing through magnificent Pine trees.
The possibilities are limitless as to the sights, sounds, sensations you
would experience. The possibilities before you are limitless.
Limitations are created by Ego-chitter chatter.
Limitations are physical realm restrictions set upon you by the conscious
mind and others to keep you in your proper place in an attempt to keep
you from soaring freely. In the Realm of Spirit there are no limitations,
for the possibilities are limitless.
All that you can conceive can be made manifest if you would but believe
it to be so.
Soar free beloved child; open your mind, your Spirit and your heart to
infinite possibilities.
All is in Divine Order as you awaken to all that surrounds you, to all that
is yet to be made manifest in physical form.
How shall you *spring* forth this day?

Day 119

CLEANSE YOUR INNER-SELF
Archangel Ariel

Beloved child, purifying, cleansing that which surrounds you does not serve your highest and best good if you do not also cleanse and purify your Inner-Spirit.

Cleanse your Inner-Spirit with prayer, meditation, walks in nature, sitting in the silence, soft gentle music, purging negative thoughts and emotions.

Do not allow all that has come before to weigh you down.

Place all that no longer serves you in a basket.

Imagine there to be a stream, set the basket upon the stream.

As the basket floats upon the stream, release the need to gaze upon the contents of what has come before.

Walk forward towards all that awaits you. Walk towards the light of my brethren and me and that of Divine Source.

Allow all that you are, your core essence, the light which shines forth to guide your way this day and all the days before you.

Day 120

PATHWAY OF HARMONY
Charmeine

~*~

Harmony is a sense of well-being, a sense of peace, a sense of joy, a sense
of bliss. Beloved child, know both your inner and outer Self.
You are whole, complete and perfect as you are in this moment and the
next, and the next.
There is nothing you need to do, need to have, or need to be, to
complete yourself, for you are already whole in all ways.
Go within, your inner core knows all, has all, sees all you could ever
desire in the Earthly realm and in the Realm of Spirit.
In the dawning of each day, there is renewal of all things.
In the setting of each day is the release of all things.
In the seeking you shall find and be found.
In the asking all shall be answered, the way smoothed before you.
In the knocking all shall be revealed to you with the opening of your
heart, mind, and Soul.
All of these are pathways to harmony.
How shall you open yourself to harmony this day?

Day 121

TRANSFORMATIONAL GRATITUDE
Emmanuel

⌒*⌒

In all things, in all places, in all ways, know you are loved; know Source
is with you always as are my brethren and I are always with you.
Know you are never alone. *Alone* is another way of saying *All One* with
God.
What is before you that you wish to have transformed?
Express gratefulness for the many gifts of love, friendship, knowledge,
abundance, for all things occurring before you.
Be open to receive that which you ask. Be open to giving that which
you ask.
Light an orange or white candle; focus upon the flame, allowing all that
no longer serves your highest and best good to be released.
Focus upon the flame of the candle; see the light of the flame illuminate
all about you. See light where darkness had been. See light open the
way before you.
Transform thoughts, emotions, your ways to reflect love and light.
Know you are loved. Know you light the way for you. Know you light
the way, seeing beyond limitations of the Earthly realm.
Expressing gratitude is an expression of thankfulness, of love, opening
your heart to receive all that you already are.
Know yourself. Know your core essence.
Know all is in Divine Order occurring in Divine Time.

Day 122

PEACEFULNESS
Melchizedek

M

Begin at the beginning.
Begin within.
Begin without.
The place you find you now is the beginning.
Breathe deeply beloved child for you are peaceful by nature.
Breathe deeply beloved child for you are an expression of perfection, you
are whole and complete as you are in this moment and the next and the
next.
Peacefulness is expressed in the release of all things, emotions, thoughts,
anger, or fear of not being where you want to be.
Allow your physical body to sigh deeply, feel your shoulders release the
burdens they carry.
Breathe deeply beloved child; you are loved beyond measure.
Breathe deeply beloved child; you are perfection.
Breathe deeply beloved child; you are peacefulness expressed in its
purest form.
Be as free as a feather floating on the gentle breeze.
Allow your Spirit to soar freely in peacefulness.
Be open to peacefulness this day and all the days before you.

Day 123

YOUR TRUE SELF
Elemiah

∽∾∽

The light within you shines brightly, radiating outward touching all
with glorious brilliance.
In your search for the path before you, look within.
All you seek is already within you this moment.
Beloved child seek within, journey within, seek first the Realm of Light
and Love.
Allow only light and love to enfold you with all you seek, all you desire.
Be willing to step into your truth, for there is no other in all the
Universe as brilliant, as you are in this moment.
Your Life's Purpose is waiting for you this moment.
Be willing to receive all you are in this moment.
Be willing to express light and love for you.
In the sharing of light and love with you, you have more than enough to
share with others.
Share the journey with other seekers of the light.
Begin within, all shall be made manifest upon your awakening.
Shine forth this day; allow your light to be a beacon in the darkness.

Day 124

HARMONY OR CHAOS
Zuriel

Harmony is a state of being; being in balance, being joyful.
If chaos surrounds you, chaos is also within you.
Harmony and chaos cannot co-exist.
That which has been made manifest before you, is that which is also within you.
If you desire peacefulness, harmony shall abide with you.
If you desire joy, harmony shall abide with you.
Look about you, how shall you choose to bring harmony into physical, emotional, mental, and Spiritual Balance?
Bringing harmony does not require massive change this instant.
Allow you to seek balance in all things, one step along your path and then another and another.
Much like spring cleaning it is time to bring you into a state of harmony.
Remove shadow and darkness, shed light within.
Light shall illuminate all that surrounds you.
Choose wisely, for in the choosing, you choose which seeds to sow within you and that which surrounds you.
What seeds shall you choose to sow this day?

Day 125

VIBRATIONAL FREEDOM
Galgaliel

The dawning of each morn begins anew with hope, faith, trust and the possibility of all things being made manifest before you.
In the dawning of each morn release all that belongs behind you.
In the dawning of each morn seek first the light and love of Source, open yourself to all that is before you.
The moment before you is all there is.
Take flight beloved child for in the freeing of your Inner-Spirit, you soar on the vibration of pure light.
Take flight, there is no other holding you from your good.
Take flight, soar among the heavens for there is only love, there is only light, there is only goodness and mercy, there is only peace and harmony.
Exchange the vibrational pattern of all that has come before.
Choose to take flight; all is in Divine Order, occurring in Divine Time.
Seek the gift presented to you in all moments from all sources, listen for there are no mistakes.
Take flight, expand your horizons, it is you who holds you where you do not want to be. Take flight; choose vibrational freedom this day and the next and the next.
Release all that no longer serves you.
How shall you choose to vibrational freedom this day?

Day 126

IGNITE YOUR INNER PASSION
Nathaniel

∼✧∼

Light the fires of passion within. Look about you, what do you see?
Look more closely. Do you see the many blessings all about you?
Perhaps you choose to look upon that which has not yet been made
manifest in physical form?
If thou do not trust in the ways of my brethren and me ... then where do
you place your trust and faith?
The higher power resides within you.
Your core essence knows only peace, harmony, light, love, abundance in
all things.
How then does one become one with Divine Source?
Sit in the silence, walk softly upon the Earth, feel the breeze upon your
skin, sing praises of gratitude, give of you to you and to others.
In the giving there is receiving.
In the receiving you give the gift of accepting the gifts of another.
Beloved child, do you give to you.
Ignite the fires of passion within.
There is nothing you cannot manifest for the asking.
There is nothing which remains closed upon knocking.
There is nothing that remains hidden in the seeking.
Choose to ignite your inner passions, choose to open yourself to receive,
choose to express gratitude for your many blessings.
Allow your Inner-Spirit to soar.
How shall you choose to express your inner passion this day?

Day 127

RELEASE LIMITING BELIEFS
Archangel Raziel

Awaken beloved child for there is much to celebrate.
Awaken for there is much to learn.
Awaken, in the awakening you are open to receiving all that you desire.
In the awakening you are open to giving of you to you.
In the awakening, there is no concept of lack; there is no concept of limitation.
Limiting beliefs serve only to hold you from your good.
Within limitation all suffer.
Discard that which seeks to keep you from your good.
Discard that which seeks to distract you from your true path.
Seek light. In seeking light there is faith, there is courage to step away from all that has come before, making clear the path before you.
Reach into you. It is you who holds you from your good, not another.
Ask and the way shall be shown to you.
Ask and the way shall be made open to you. Ask and it shall be given to you.

SPIRITUAL ALCHEMY
Archangel Metatron

M

Alchemy is the changing of lead into gold.
Imagine for a moment transforming your energy from lead into gold.
Beloved child, lead represents all that has brought you to this moment,
all that has come before, all that no longer serves your highest and best
good.
Gold is the light which pours in through your Crown chakra,
illuminating all within you, radiating outward as a beacon in the
darkness.
Lead is negativity made manifest in your thoughts, emotions, in your
actions.
Be willing to release that which no longer serves you.
Be willing to release the need to burden yourself with leaden thoughts,
emotions, actions.
Be willing to release and surrender to loving thoughts, emotions, actions.
In the releasing, you allow transformation. You open yourself to
Spiritual Alchemy transforming your Inner-Self in ways yet to be made
known to your Human self.
Step into the light.
Step into your true self.
Turn the lead of all that has come before into gold opening the way
before you.

HEAVEN ON EARTH
Gamaliel

Your thoughts are your life.
Your life is a reflection of your thoughts.
That which you think about becomes your reality.
Your reality is a reflection of your thoughts.
Your thoughts create emotions.
Your thoughts and emotions create actions.
Thoughts, emotions, actions are a reflection of all that has brought you to this moment. Choose different thoughts.
Thoughts create the world about you.
Fill your thoughts with grace, grace shall abide within.
Fill your mind and heart with love and light, love and light shall abide within.
You need not change everything in one moment as this shall not be everlasting.
Choose first one thought and then another, and another.
Express gratitude for the many blessings about you this moment.
Gratitude creates within you a sense of harmony.
Harmony creates a sense of peacefulness.
How shall you create Heaven on Earth this day?

Day 130

SELF-EMPOWERMENT
Guardian Angel of Power

⁓⁓⁓

Breathe deeply, exhale slowly ... breathe deeply, exhale slowly.
Calm your mind, still your thoughts.
Feel this moment come to life.
There is only this moment there is no other.
Seek the light and love within; there is no power greater than the light
of Divine Source. There is no power greater than the light which shines
from within you this moment. Become a beacon for yourself.
Illuminate all before you; accept all that has come before for it delivered
you to where you find yourself along your path.
Look forward; focus upon where you choose to be.
Seek first illumination within.
Light the way for you, no other can light the way for you.
Look to the light beloved child for all is indeed in Divine Order.
If what you see, hear, feel, does not please you, choose differently.
In the choosing you empower you.
How shall you choose to celebrate empowering you?

Day 131

GRACE WITHIN
Muriel

⌒✼⌒

Take comfort for that which is before you is in Divine Order, occurring
with Divine Timing. It may at first appear as though that which faces
you is a test, a hurdle to overcome.
Call upon me to soften your thoughts. Open your heart, allowing the
gift of grace to flow within, radiating outward creating a sense of peace
and harmony.
The ego voice encourages thoughts based in fear ... lack of time, lack of
money, lack of love, fear of being alone, fear of not having enough.
We remind you gently there is only love and light, all else need not
concern you. You may find yourself in a place where you do not want to be.
Do you truly desire to reside in harmony, peacefulness, abundance and
prosperity, loving compassion, in a state of grace?
Change how you see people, places, and things and what you see will change.
Change your thoughts and what you think about changes.
Change how you feel in this moment and this moment changes.
Changing one thought, one emotion, one action transforms everything
within and all that surrounds you.
There is much to be thankful for now this moment. Start where you are,
lovingly place one foot in front of the other along the path before you.
See through the eyes of love and light, all shall be made manifest before you.
Allow love and light to illuminate all before you, releasing shadow and
fear to the light. Offer no resistance, all shall flow around you with grace
and ease.
Gracefully allow all to do, be or have that which they choose for themselves.
Gracefully allow you the choice to be, do or have that which you desire.
Gifts of love, harmony and peace are gifts of grace.

Day 132

ACCEPTANCE OF YOUR TRUTH
Omniel

Close your eyes step into your mind, imagine there is a slight breeze
gently brushing against your skin.
Listen, what do you hear?
Perhaps a babbling brook ... birds singing ... children playing ... thunder
in the distance? Perhaps you detect the scent of rain.
In the instant you sense, hear, or see, you experience Oneness with
Divine Source.
All things are energy.
Energy vibrates on many levels in many ways.
Bring you into balance.
Bring you into harmony.
Bring to you peacefulness.
All these and more are Oneness, Oneness with Source.
There are many paths towards that which you seek.
There are many experiences upon the path before you. There is only
One Source.
Step into the light beloved child for all is given to you in the asking.
Open your heart, open your mind.
Open the door before you.
All waits for you to beckon to you acceptance of your truth.

Day 133

PIVOT TOWARDS THE LIGHT
Ohrmazd

~M~

Beloved child, you are the light.
You are a beacon in the darkness.
Call upon my brethren and me, we shall cast out shadow and darkness
infilling every place with Source light and love.
You are whole, complete, and perfect now, this moment.
There is no other needed to complete you.
There is no other needed, for you are loved beyond measure.
Love is the answer to all things.
It may appear as though shadow and darkness will overtake you.
Pivot towards the light.
Pivot towards loving thoughts, loving actions, loving emotions.
You need only place one foot in front of the other.
Seek first the light within you.
There is nothing that cannot be illuminated.
Allow your wounds to heal and be healed.
Give us your cares, concerns, worries.
You are whole, complete and perfect now, this moment.
How shall you choose to pivot towards the light this day?

Day 134

SEEING PAST ILLUSION
Zachriel

⟶

See beyond self-made limitations.
Limitation is taught by others, reinforced by the conscious mind.
Limitation is fear based thought which no longer serves your highest
and best good. Limitation is a perception of not being, doing, or having
all that you desire.
Be willing to see past the illusion of lack, limitation.
Step into the light, remember who you are.
You are light.
You are love expressed fully, without hesitation.
There is only love or fear.
Do you choose to remember loving thoughts, situations, experiences?
Yes, acknowledge all that has come before, for it has brought you to this
moment.
We ask you see past the limitation of what was, seeing past perceived
illusion.
Step into the light, bringing into harmony and balance all that you
already are with who you have allowed you to become along the journey.
In any moment you are free to choose to remain in the shadows of what
was or step into the light of what is.
Look about for there is much to be thankful for.
Look about, seeing past illusion, stepping into the warmth of love and
light.
All is well, go in peace this day.

Day 135

RENEWAL, REGENERATION
Israfil

⌒*⌒

Rise from all that has come before this moment.
Rise from all perceived pain and sorrow.
Rise from the ashes of what was, giving thanks for what is yet to be.
Raise your voice in thanksgiving for all is made manifest before you for
the asking.
Seek answers in prayer, meditation, in the silence.
Seek not the ways of judgment lest you be judged.
Seek not the ways of days long past.
Seek instead the light and love of Divine Source.
Infill the body, mind and Soul with thanksgiving for in this moment all
is made new again.
Give thanksgiving for the regeneration of the body, mind and Soul for
in so doing, you are made whole.
Each breath brings into the physical being life giving energy, renewing
your Spirit.
Each breath brings the promise of something more.
Each breath brings the promise of rising from all that no longer serves
your highest and best good.
Each breath brings the promise of renewal.
Breathe deeply; renew your Spirit.
Breathe deeply; renew your Inner-Self with love and light, healing all
that has come before clearing the way before you.
Breathe deeply this day giving thanks for blessings great and small.
Breathe deeply this day.

Day 136

GIVING THANKS
Emmanuel

⌐₥⌐

In all things be grateful.
In all creatures both great and small, be grateful. In all faces, in all places
be grateful.
Gratitude is an expression of giving thanks.
Giving thanks for all miracles, for all blessings, for all gifts given you are
cause for celebration.
In celebrating all that has come before and all that is before you, the way
is made clear. Seek first gratitude for the many blessings in your life this
moment, for there is much to be thankful for.
In reaching for grace within, grace shall dance in celebration all about
and within you. Breathe deeply, for all is in Divine Order occurring in
Divine Time.
No person, thing, no situation is pre-destined.
There are many choices along the journey.
How you choose to travel upon the path before you is your choice and
your choice alone. Yes, along the way there are many encounters, many
opportunities.
At times that which appears to be a distraction, is a gift of
transformation of all that has come before, bringing you to what is.
In choosing, there is freedom to transform all that no longer serves your
highest and best good.
Begin where you are; give thanks for all things, for all places, for all
creatures.
Become as the caterpillar; allow all that has come before to transform
you into your true self ... spread your wings in thanks giving.

Day 137

DISCERNMENT
Jaoel

~*~

All is in the choosing beloved child.
There are countless ways to travel the journey before you.
Do you seek guidance as to which path and how best to travel that
which lay before you?
Call upon me, light 3 white candles, settle yourself.
Ask to be shown the way.
All shall be revealed in the asking.
Do you seek to know your Life Purpose?
All shall be revealed in the asking.
Do you seek ways in which to live your Life Purpose more fully?
All shall be reveled in the asking.
Choose among the countless choices.
It is in the choosing all shall be made manifest before you.
Be willing to see past perceived limitation.
Be willing to see past that which may displease or frighten you.
Be willing to open your heart with compassion for yourself.
The journey is not the goal; the journey is the culmination of all
experiences both positive and negative.
All that is yet to be made manifest is but awaiting you.
Choose wisely with compassion, for in choosing, you choose the path
before you.

Day 138

STATE OF GRACE AND HARMONY
Archangel Haniel

Sit in the silence; allow the stillness to surround you.
Sit in the silence; allow the stillness to enter the physical body, filling
your entire being, softly extending outward into all your energy bodies.
Be open to the stillness, open your mind, open your heart.
Stillness is the silence in between thoughts, between emotions, between
actions. Stillness is a state of grace, harmony, a state of peacefulness.
Allow your physical body to release all its burdens real or perceived.
In the releasing the body becomes lighter, the Spirit becomes brighter.
In the releasing, you create space for loving thoughts, emotions, and
actions.
In the releasing, you create a state of grace and harmony.
Open to all that is before you with grace.
All is before you; reach out to me and my brethren, for we are
messengers of Source.
Step into the light; be in a state of harmony all this day.
Grace and harmony shall be your constant companion.

Day 139

GIFT OF IMAGINATION
Guardian Angel of Gifts

⌒◊⌒

All that you are all that you have and all that you do was made manifest
first through thoughts and from moments now behind you.
All that you are, all that you have, and all that you do from this moment
forward is made manifest through thought and emotion.
Do you desire to have, be or do things differently?
Begin where you are, imagine the way you see all things for yourself.
Imagine there are no limitations.
Imagine you can be, do or have anything your heart desires. Your true
desires are rays of light and love, radiating within.
Seek first peace and serenity within.
Seek first harmony and balance within.
All shall be made manifest before you.
The way is made clear for all you desire and more.
The way is made clear, are you open to receiving all that you seek?
Are you open to receiving all that you ask? Are you prepared for the
open door before you? Are you open to Divine Source?
Open your heart, open your mind, open your Inner-Spirit, nothing is
denied you.
The miracle is in the giving and in the receiving.
To receive, one must give from the heart.
To give, one must be able to receive with an open heart. Where shall
you journey this day?
Allow your thoughts and emotions to create all that you desire and more.
Peace be with you. You are loved beyond measure all the days of your
life.

Day 140

TRUST THE RADIANCE WITHIN
Archangel Uriel

Light shines down upon you. Light shines within you.
Light radiates from your Inner-Essence, touching all who come into
your thoughts, touching all you see, touching all things everywhere in
every dimension.
That which is given to you by Source cannot be darkened cannot be
contained, nor can it be extinguished by mankind.
That which is given to you cannot be taken from you
That which is given to you cannot be imprisoned by another's thoughts,
actions nor emotions.
It is you and only you which can do these things to your Inner-
Radiance.
Trust the light given to you by Source.
Trust the light within, it shall shed light upon all in the physical realm.
There is only truth, love and light which shines forth through the
radiance within.
Trust the radiance within, it shall cast out shadow and doubt
illuminating all before you in grace, in harmony.
Seek counsel in physical form. There are those among you who have
great knowledge, great light, those who judge you not.
Call upon me and my brethren to illuminate the path before you this day.
Step into the light, feel the warmth upon your skin. Look about you, for
in truth there is only love and light.
Trust the radiance within given you by Divine Source and of the Angelic
Realm.
Trust ....

Day 141

SERENITY
Angel of Serenity

Allow you to release sorrow, pain, conflict, un-ease, dis-ease. Allow you
to release all that rises from fear based thoughts and fear based
emotions.
Disengage from struggle and conflict.
Simply allow you to be drawn into the light of Divine Source.
There is only light, there is only love.
All else is an attempt to distract you from your path along the journey
before you.
There are many paths to that which you seek.
Seek first the light within you for the light within, is the seed from
Divine Source.
Seek first the light within.
Your core essence is tranquil, peaceful, joyful.
Open yourself to that which creates within you a sense of peace and
tranquility.
You need not look behind you; begin where you are, acknowledging all
that has come before.
Give you the gift of being open to receiving all that you seek, all you
desire.
Light a candle, sit in the silence, allowing guidance to be given to you in
the silence.
How shall you choose serenity this day?

Day 142

TRANSFORMATIONAL TRUTHS
Angel of Power

⌒ᴍ⌒

The power of Divine Love and Light is within you.
The power of Divine Love and Light is within all creatures, within all things.
The power of Divine Love and Light enfolds all creatures, all things.
The power of Divine Love and Light is gentle in its strength.
The power of Divine Love and Light illuminates all people, places, situations.
The power of Divine Love and Light is to be used wisely, with integrity.
Are you willing to allow Divine Love and Light to cast out negativity, purify intentions within you and towards others?
Are you willing to allow Divine Love and Light to transform you within?
Are you willing to receive all that you seek?
Are you willing to release that which does not serve you?
Are you willing to release judgment?
Are you willing to forgive yourself and all others for wrongs, real or perceived?
Are you willing to go within, *seeing* with clarity?
Are you willing to open yourself to these transformational truths before you?
How shall you choose to use gifts given to you this day?

Day 143

LISTEN, SEEING TRUTH
Angel of Discernment

Listen to your inner voice.
Listen to whispers upon the breeze.
Listen to inner guidance, knowing that which is for your highest and best good is being revealed to you.
Listen to the stirrings in your heart.
Listen, for in listening all is revealed.
That which is before you this moment is filled with emotion, thought, action.
That which is before you this moment is filled with appearances filtered through all that brought to where you are.
Open your inner sight; open your inner sense of Self.
See through the eyes of Divine Love and Grace.
The truth shall be revealed to you in the seeking.
Each footfall upon the path along the journey is a choice.
How shall you choose to honor yourself, others, truth, light and love this day?

REACH FOR THE STARS
Guardian Angels of Peace and Light

There are many choices, many paths along the journey before you.
Reach for the Stars. Release that which attempts to distract you from all
that you desire. Step into the Light of Divine Source for truth,
righteousness, love, peace, forgiveness and harmony shall accompany
you all your days.
All is given to you in the asking.
All is given to you in the releasing of all that has come before.
All is given to you in the releasing of shadow or darkness.
Step into the Light feel the warmth within.
Close your eyes, feel the gentle warmth begin to expand within your
entire being.
Allow the Light to shine forth from within, expanding with each
breathe.
Step into the Light beloved child, all is revealed in the silence.
All is revealed in the Light.
All is revealed in the release of all that no longer serves your highest and
best good. Freedom awaits you, freedom to choose differently, freedom
to focus upon this moment, freedom to choose peace.
Reach for the Stars, step into the Light.

Day 145

STEP INTO THE LIGHT
Ananchel

Each step along the path before you is filled with many choices,
distractions, light and love.
Each step along the path before you brings the gift of choice.
The gift in choosing is before you this present moment.
Perhaps there is something or someone before you this moment.
Perhaps that which has come before this moment tempts to pull you
from where you are, from where you want to be, back to where you have
already been.
Breathe deeply, exhale all doubt.
Breathe deeply; exhale all shadows of what once was.
Breathe deeply inhaling light and love. Exhale all that has come before.
Breathe deeply, feel your entire being release all that is not of light,
release all that is not of love.
Open your heart, mind, your Soul to all that awaits you in the light.
Step into the light, release you from all that has come before this
moment.
Step into the light beloved child.

Day 146

JOURNEYING THE PATH BEFORE YOU
Micah

⏤

Beloved child all is well.

All is in Divine Order according to Divine Plan, occurring in Divine Time.

This is not to say you do not have choices. There are always choices before you.

The Divine Purpose for you is part of the overall Divine Plan for all creatures great and small.

Traveling the path along the journey before you is not pre-determined.

There are countless ways to journey the path before you.

At times you shall travel among lush forests, beside babbling brooks or roaring rivers. At other times you will rest, gathering your energy for the journey as it is being revealed.

It may appear at times as though you may be stepping backwards.

It is in these moments choices made are the greatest.

For in choosing, you travel back along whence you came, stay where you are, or forge ahead to all that awaits you.

Seek first your Inner-Guidance, that which resonates within, in peace and harmony, happiness and joy.

That which does not resonate within does not serve your highest and best good.

Choose wisely, choose in love and light.

All shall be revealed in the asking.

All is made manifest before you.

All is well.

Go in peace this day.

Day 147

BE WILLING TO SEE PAST APPEARANCES
Archangel Raphael

Open your eyes open your heart, open your mind.
Be willing to see past appearances.
Be willing to see past perception.
Be willing to forgive yourself.
Be willing to forgive others.
All creatures great and small travel the path before them.
All creatures great and small travel the path before them as it unfolds.
Each unfolding, provides an opportunity to choose.
In the choosing, there is harmony or dis-harmony.
The choosing belongs to you and only you.
All that has come before this moment has brought you to where you are.
All that you choose in this moment delivers you to that which is before you.
Allow yourself the gift of seeing, feeling, thinking, choosing with clarity.
Call upon me; open your heart, mind, body, and Soul to healing from within.
Call upon me to illuminate the path before you.
Call upon me to assist you this day.
All is well for there is only love and light.
How shall you choose to *see* this day?

Day 148

INNER LIGHT
Archangel Zadkiel

To yourself be true. To yourself be love. To yourself be forgiving.
All lies within you this moment. Release you from all that has brought
you to this moment for it no longer serves your highest and best good.
To yourself be true. Look within, what do you *see*?
Do you *see* love and light, or do you *see* shadow and darkness?
The choice is yours. The choice has, and always will be yours and yours
alone.
Be willing to *see* the Divine Spark within you this moment, it is within
you.
In what ways have you allowed your Inner Light, the Divine Spark
within to become dull and lifeless?
Are you willing to practice faith, gratitude, compassion and mercy?
Seek first the light within. The outer physical Self is a reflection of the
Inner-Self.
That which is within you radiates outward.
That which is made manifest in the outer physical realm is a reflection
of that which is within your thoughts, your heart, your emotions.
In the choosing all is made manifest.
How shall you choose to manifest for you this day?

HOPE
Archangel Remiel

Hope is eternal. Love is eternal. Light is eternal.
The path before you is never ending. The path before you unfolds with
each breath, each thought, each sensation, each heartfelt emotion.
There is no wrong or right decision. There are simply choices,
opportunities to expand your Inner-Spiritual Self, expanding yourself in
the outer physical realm.
In all things there must be balance, joy, harmony.
In seeking these things all shall unfold before you with grace and ease.
All is shown to you in ways not yet imagined. All is given to you in ways
unforeseen.
All is made manifest in the Earthly realm as it is made manifest in the
Realm of spirit. Be merciful and mercy shall accompany you all your
days. Give first to you; in giving to you, you create an abundance of all
things.
In giving to yourself, you create overflowing joy, happiness, love,
radiating Source Light from within.
The well of all things begins within, overflowing outward into physical
manifestation. Seek first the light within, light shall be made manifest
before you illuminating all things, casting out doubt and fear, casting out
shadow and darkness.
There is only light. There is only love. Hope springs eternal. Love is
eternal. Light is eternal.
How shall you choose to journey the path before you this day?

Day 150

BALANCE IN ALL THINGS
Camael

⌒✳⌒

Balance in all things brings peacefulness, harmony, joy.
Balance in all things opens the path before you in harmony.
Balance in all things clears the path before you, illuminating all
perception of shadow and darkness.
Balance in all things creates opportunities for loving yourself and others.
Balance in all things creates opportunities of increased prosperity,
abundance, Spirituality, quiet, laughter, joy, a deeper sense of love.
In all things seek balance within; balance shall be made manifest in all
around you. Your innate wisdom shall guide you without fail.
Focus not upon that which creates harm within your thoughts, your
heart.
Focus not upon fear based thoughts.
Focus upon that which creates peace, harmony, joy.
At the edge of everything you have ever known, step out into the
unknown for there will be stones to support thee or you shall be given
wings to fly.

Day 151

HEALING BEGINS WITHIN
Archangel Jeremiel

Healing begins with your inner core, your true essence of light and love.
All thoughts, emotions and actions are based in fear or in love.
It matters not the way in which fear rises be it cloaked in shadow,
doubt, or lack.
All are laced with fear.
Love is calm, peaceful, happy, joyous, prosperous, opening yourself to
endless possibilities.
Love encourages stepping forth to all which awaits you.
Love encourages you to open yourself by preparing to receive all that
you desire.
Call upon me and my brethren, we shall assist you in conducting a most
loving life review, acknowledging all that has brought you to this
moment.
You need not be harsh or judgmental with yourself. Be gentle, loving,
nurturing yourself as you acknowledge all that has come before.
Light a purple candle; surround you with amethyst purple light.
You have prepared for all that awaits you.
Step into the light beloved child for there is only love, there is only light.
Step out onto the path before you with faith, trust.
Open your heart, mind, your Soul, embracing all that awaits you.
Step into the light ....

Day 152

INTERWOVEN CONNECTEDNESS
Archangel Haniel

Know your true Inner-Essence. Know your thoughts, your emotions.
All that is made manifest in the physical realm is a reflection of knowing
your Inner-Self.
Your core essence is peacefulness, harmony, joy.
Balance the outer physical self with the Inner-Self. In seeking your
Inner-Self, a sense of knowing expands within you.
The expansion of light and love create within and without a stronger
connection with Divine Source.
In reality there is no separation between Divine Source and all that is
made manifest in the physical realm.
It is Ego-chitter chatter creates the illusion of separation. All things, all
places, all of humankind is connected with one another, interwoven
through Divine Source.
There is no separation; there is only connection with Divine Source and
the Angelic Realm. Call upon me and my brethren, we shall open your
inner pathways to all that you are, for you are whole, complete and
perfect now this moment.
How shall you choose to experience peace and harmony this day?

Day 153

COMFORT AND JOY
Angel of Eternal Love

⌒*ᴍ*⌒

Tidings beloved Child of God.
We bring tidings of comfort and joy.
There is much joy within and around you.
Look about around you this moment.
What do your physical eyes see?
What does your physical body feel or sense?
What thoughts sift through your mind?
What emotions are you experiencing this moment?
Love is eternal, ever flowing, un-ceasing.
Limitation is a perception of lack.
Divine Source knows not of limitation, nor boundaries that confine the
Spirit.
For there is no lack, there is only the pure expression of infinite, un-
conditional love. There is only abundance, prosperity, health, joy,
compassion, harmony.
Love is eternal.
Open your heart, giving love to you.
Open your heart, giving love to others.
In the giving, there is receiving. In the receiving there is giving.
How shall you express love you and for others this day?
Go forth this day beloved Child of Divine Source in love this day.
Comfort and joy shall be your constant companions.

Day 154

INVOKE AN INNER AWAKENING
Archangel Zadkiel

⌒ᴍ⌒

Invoke the spark of Divinity within.
Invoke the light of Divine Source within your heart-center.
Awaken the Divine Nature within.
Awaken your true essence.
Awaken your entire being to wondrous unconditional love, acceptance,
trust, faith, nurturing you with gentleness and mercy all your days.
Call upon me to guide you this day and all days before you.
The wisdom of your Divine Nature shall be your constant companion
for all your days.

Day 155

GARDEN OF EDEN WITHIN
Cathetel

Attune yourself with the Divine Nature within you.
Tend your inner Spiritual garden of peace, love, joy, hope, faith and trust.
The approaching storm simply passes you by for in the garden, there is only love and light.
Within all creatures, within all of humankind the seed sparks eternal.
How do you tend your Spiritual garden?
Do you seek to release the seeds of discontent?
Do you plant seeds of light, prosperity, happiness, harmony and peacefulness?
All that is within you is made manifest all about you.
Tend your inner Spiritual garden well, for you are whole, complete and perfect. The Garden of Eden is within you.

Day 156

UNTOLD BLESSINGS AWAIT YOU
Barakiel

Ⓜ

How shall you choose to rejoice this day?
Wherever you are in this moment, how do you choose to see you?
Do you choose to look upon that which has yet to be made manifest?
Or perhaps you choose to look upon the many blessings all about you
this moment, giving thanks for all that is made manifest before you.
In giving thanks for the place, situation, or relationship in which you
find yourself, you clear the way to manifest that which you desire most.
In rejoicing for all there is, all that you are, and all that you have, you
begin to resonate with untold blessings which await you.
This place in which you find yourself is the sum of all that has come
before.
How shall you create that which you desire most?
Seek the light within, expressing heartfelt gratitude and appreciation for
the many blessings all about you now this moment.

Day 157

INFINITES POSSIBILITIES
Archangel Raguel

~*~

Within your Inner-Self, your core essence there is limitless light
illuminating all about you.
Within you lay infinite possibilities.
There is nothing you cannot have, cannot be, cannot do.
There is nothing denied you.
As you dream so can it be.
As you dare to open you, to all that lay before you, previous boundaries
expand providing a greater sense of freedom in the place you now find
yourself Spiritual, mentally, emotionally and physically.
It is Ego-chitter chatter in the physical realm which binds you to all that
has come before.
Dare to dream, dare to step beyond that which has come before, dare to
step into the light seeing infinite possibilities all about you.
Dare to dream, dare to see, dare to feel, dare to hear, dare to sense.
Dare to breathe in all you desire.

Day 158

HEALING FROM WITHIN
Archangel Raphael

Ask and it shall be granted.
What is before you or within you which seeks to be healed?
All that is made manifest in the body is a symptom of that which seeks
to be healed.
If you harbor anger, frustration, any fear base thought or emotion it is
manifested in your physical body, in the energy which surrounds you
and in experiences.
All is based in fear or in love.
We do not suggest turning a blind eye to all that is not of love.
Observe, acknowledging that which is a truth for another, for there is
always choice. You are free to choose to accept your truth or the truth of
another for you.
In the choosing, there is freedom from all that does not resonate within
you.
In the choosing there is freedom to choose health and well-being.
In so much as you believe, so shall you be healed.

Day 159

SPEAK WITH LOVE AND COMPASSION
Jeduthun

Light a candle, sing praises of glory to the Creator of all there is.
Light a candle; allow your inner truth to flow freely from your heart and
tongue.
In all you do, think, feel, say ... speak from your heart with gentleness
and compassion for you alone have the power to speak with love or
malice.
Speak from your heart. If there are no words, allow your heart to express
through when words fail you.
Seek within you solace, musings, peace, joy.
For in the seeking you shall find all you desire and more.
Light the path before you with love and grace.
Love and grace shall accompany you all your days.

BE NOT AFRAID
Archangel Michael

Call upon me and my brethren, we shall clear the way before you.
All is cast in the light of everlasting love.
All that is not of love shall be cast aside.
All that is not for your highest and best good has no dominion over you.
All that is not of love and light shall fall from you in the asking.
All shall be granted to you, for you are a beloved child of Divine Source.
All shall be granted to you, for you are loved beyond measure.
Call upon me to protect you from thoughts, intentions, emotions of those who would seek to harm you.
Call upon me to clear your path.
Call upon me to cleanse your entire being of all that is not of love and light, all that is not for your highest and best good.
All is well, all is in Divine Order.
All is made whole in the asking.
Know this is so now, this moment.
Go in peace; know you are cloaked within my great wings of protection, unconditional love, light and mercy.
Be not afraid this day for you are cleansed of all that no longer serves you.

Day 161

INNER WISDOM, INNER TRUTH
Archangel Zadkiel

Know you this day.
Seek first the light within you, for all is illuminated with your inner
wisdom.
Your inner wisdom is that of Divine Source.
Your inner wisdom resonates from deep within, from your core essence.
You shall know your truth.
Wisdom shall set you free from all judgments, from lack, from all that is
not of love. Listen with your inner ears.
Open yourself to hearing, feeling, sensing your inner truth.
All is before you this day.
Balance and harmony are your innate gifts.
Know you this day.

Day 162

INNER PEACE, SELF-LOVE
Archangel Chamuel

Love yourself as you would love others.
Love yourself openly, gently, with compassion.
All that has come before this moment brought you to where you are.
Embrace all that faces you.
Nurture you with loving-kindness for you are whole, complete, and
perfect this moment. There is nothing to re-arrange.
There is nothing to surrender.
There is nothing that needs to be done or un-done.
Your core essence is your true self.
Allow you inner light to shine forth this day radiating peace, harmony,
joy.

IN THE MOMENT OF THE ASKING
Archangel Gabriel

There are many about you who would see you silenced.
There are many about you who would see your sight blinded.
Many about you would attempt to hold you where you have already traveled.
In the seeking of your true essence, be not swayed by thoughts, emotions, deeds, intentions of others.
Call upon me and my brethren, we shall assist you in the moment of the asking.
Call upon me and my brethren, we shall light the way before you.
Call upon me and my brethren, we shall make the way smooth before you.
Be strong in the days ahead, all is given in the moment of the asking.
Allow yourself to align with all you have asked.
Step out of your own way.
Gift yourself with your heart's desires.
Peace be with you this day and all the days before you.

Day 164

CELEBRATE
Cama'el

~ *M* ~

Celebrate joy, harmony, peace.
Contentment shall be your constant companion.
Celebrate the many blessings, gifts given you.
Celebrate the abundance of opportunities.
Choose to see that which is gifted to you rather than the absence of your desires.
All is in Divine Time occurring in Divine Order.
Choose to see past the illusion of lack for in reality there is no lack there is only abundance in all things.
Choose to see past illusion for the ways of the physical realm do not bind you.
Choose to see love, feel love, express love.
That which is not expressed in its fullest is lost to you and those around you.
That which is not expressed in thought, emotion, through your actions is forever lost. Choose to express your Divine Nature for in sharing, you prepare yourself to receive all you seek.
Celebrate the many joys this day.
Celebrate the many gifts given you.
Contentment shall be your constant companion.

Day 165

FAITH IN THE INTERNAL
Uzziel

∽✳✳✳∼

Faith ... how do you perceive a virtue such as faith?
Do you perceive a testing, a trial, lessons perhaps? Faith, an elusive virtue
of patience; mercy, compassion, love, forgiveness, acceptance, gentleness
are all expressions of faith. That which faces you this moment, do you
have faith that all is in Divine Order?
Do you practice the virtues of faith within your thoughts?
Do you first practice the art of loving yourself?
In the loving of you, there is an abundance of love, an abundance of faith
in all its many facets to share with another.
In the practicing of faith, we remind you the perception of being tested
is an Earthly realm concept. Radiate love.
Imagine sending forth soft loving rose light ... wrap yourself in rose
light allowing you to feel being filled with unconditional love, joy,
contentment.
Imagine soft loving rose light enfolding someone close to you; breathe
in soft rose light ... exhale shadow and darkness.
For shadow and darkness would steal from you all your deepest desires.
In the face of that which appears to be confrontational is the perception
on the part of another or is there a shift within you signifying disruption
within a known comfort zone. This we say to you ... go within, become
peaceful, radiate love, radiate kindness, radiate the light of Divine
Source, for all is occurring in Divine Time, in Divine Order.
Seek first peace within. Peace shall radiate outward touching all with
your thoughts, actions, emotions.
Faith, how do you practice the gift of faith this day?

ALLOW YOUR VOICE TO BE HEARD
Jeduthun

The sound of your voice is sweet music to all the Heavens.
The sound of your voice brings forth sounds of gratitude.
The sound of your voice is reassuring to all around you.
The sound of your voice is love expressed.
The sound of your voice lifts your desires from possibility to reality in
the physical realm, for it is already made manifest in Realm of Spirit.
Raise your voice, allow you to be heard .
We do not say shout your desires, we say instead raise your voice so that
you may hear yourself speak aloud.
Speak aloud in soft, loving tones giving life to all your desires.
Release all your desires to the heavens.
Call upon me and my brethren, we shall accompany you in a most
glorious choir singing songs of praise, gratitude, love, giving thanks for
the multitude of blessings gifted you. Allow your voice to be heard this
day.

Day 167

DIVINE SOURCE ENERGY
Guardian Angel of Power

⟳

Divine Love enfolds you this moment.
Divine Love enfolds you all your days.
Divine Source Energy is within you, enfolding you, moving through you, radiating outward from your core essence.
Close your eyes breathe deeply inhaling light and love into your entire being.
Exhale all perceived shadow and darkness for there is only light, there is only love. Release all that no longer serves your good.
Release fear for it cannot sustain you.
Release shadow for there is no light in the darkness of fear, there is only lack.
Open your heart, open your mind, open your Spirit to all which awaits you.
All your desires, all your dreams await you in physical form for all is made manifest in the moment of the asking in the Realm of Spirit.
How shall you choose to honor your power?
How shall you choose to align yourself and that of your dreams with Divine Source?

STAY TRUE TO YOU
Abdiel and Ongkanon

That which is before you seeks only to strengthen you for your highest
and best good. That which is before you seeks to bring you into the
light, enfolding you in the eternal love of Divine Source.
Become still in the silence, listen with your heart, your ears, your Soul.
Reach deep within you.
Practice faith for all is well this day and all the days before you.
Reach deep within you, dear one for you are whole, complete and
perfect now, this moment.
Call upon us; we shall accompany you all your days.
Call upon us; we shall weave harmony, peace, joy, abundance and
prosperity all about and within you.

Day 169

EXPANDING BEYOND YOUR COMFORT ZONE
Archangel Haniel

⌒*✧*⌒

All that has come before this moment brings you to the edge of all you
have known. There is much growth, much expansion before you.
There are a few among you who would see you stand your ground,
expanding no further. We say this to you ... place one foot before the
other, step into the light, come out of the shadows for there is only love
and light, compassion, strength, harmony and balance, abundance and
prosperity, seeing beyond physical realm limitations.
There is much which tempts you from your path.
Give you the gift of reaching out to another to assist you in your
Spiritual growth.
Choose wisely seeking the Soul Light of another whose gift of light is
unconditional. Trusting the path before you may at times be fraught
with the appearance of deceit. This we say to you, all that is not of love
and light shall be made known to you.
Give thanks, for the light shines upon all things in all places great and
small.
All is illuminated in the light of Source.
There is only light.
There is only love.
All else shall fall from you.
Be not afraid this day.

Day 170

COURAGE TO HEAL
Archangel Raphael

There is much which surrounds you that is not of love and light. In all things heal your Inner-Self from all that is now behind you.
That which is behind you, has brought you to where you are in this moment.
Celebrate; give thanks where you are for it shall be your stepping stone to all that is before you.
Look within; discover your Divine Spark of Divinity. Your Inner-Spirit is whole, complete, perfection. Your Inner-Spirit needs nothing, no one outside itself, for all things, all needs, al desires await you in the Realm of Spirit.
Your physical being seeks healing, comfort, love, joy, abundance, forgiveness, compassion, acceptance.
Know you are all things to yourself and to all who surround you this moment.
Choose to heal your Inner-Self.
Choose to release all that no longer serves you.
Choose to step into the light of forgiveness. Stepping into the light creates a sense of freedom, releasing the heavy burdens you carry within your heart.
Burdens, real or perceived, do not aid you in the seeking of happiness and joy.
In reaching for joy in all things, great and small, align with yourself in the light, in oneness, for in truth there is no separation from your core essence of love and light and that of your physical self.
Your core essence is always connected with Divine Source.

In truth you are always connected with your Inner-Spirit, always connected with your Higher Self and that of Divine Source. Choose healing.

Choose peace and harmony. Choose light.

Choose to love you. Choose courage.

FREEDOM AND GRACE
Archangel Zadkiel

⌒*⌒

This moment is filled with grace. This moment is filled with freedom.
Freedom to choose as grace guides your footsteps along the path before
you.
Can you not breathe as deeply, loudly, or as softly as you desire? Can you
not focus your energy in whichever way pleases you? Can you not
choose to love or hate?
How then can you say, feel or think you do not have freedom to choose?
If you believe there is no freedom, so be it, it shall be your truth.
If you believe there is freedom to choose, to be, to do, to manifest all
your heart's desires, so be it, it shall be your truth.
All is granted to you in the moment of asking. Ask and it shall be
granted.
Do you desire healing? Ask it and healing shall be given.
Believe, for it is already so in the Realm of Spirit.
Ask for to health be restored, beginning with your inner core essence.
Ask for health to be restored in your cells, blood, heart, mind, Soul, in
all your energy bodies.
Be willing to accept gifts given to you.
For in truth there is only love, health, abundance, light, faith, joy, peace,
wisdom, discernment, harmony and serenity.
All else is physical realm perception.
How shall you choose this day?
Go in peace for you are loved and cared for beyond measure.

Day 172

SEEDS OF YOUR HEART'S DESIRES
Cathetel

⁓卐⁓

You have planted many seeds. Do you tend to seeds which have
planted?
How do you tend your inner garden, your heart's desires?
Do you water your seeds with love, trust, faith?
Your seeds, your heart's desires require tending. Your inner garden is a
precious gift. Your inner garden is a gift from Divine Source.
You inner garden is a reflection of that which is made manifest in
physical form.
Do you dig-up the seeds having been planted with heart-felt desire
checking for growth? Have faith, trust knowing the seeds of your heart's
desires shall be made manifest. Imagine the seeds you have sown, begin
to manifest before you.
In all things give thanks for in giving thanks all is made manifest.
Tend your garden this day with love, faith, joy, harmony ... trusting all is
occurring in Divine Order, arriving in Divine Time.
Look about you this day. Open your eyes, heart, Soul, mind and your
Spirit for there is nothing denied you except by you.
Tend your garden with joy, harmony, trust ... with faith this day.

Day 173

FREEDOM OF EXPRESSION
Angel of Creativity

Know there is nothing you need to do, to be, or to have that would then complete you, for you are whole, complete, and perfect now this moment and all moments before you. How do you choose to see you? Do you choose to see that which has yet to be made manifest in physical form?

Do you choose to express yourself with loving compassion?

Do you choose to create your heart's desires?

How do you choose to create your heart's desires?

Light a candle; or perhaps write your heart's desires upon paper, the telling of a different, positive, loving and abundant story.

Bring life to that which you desire most ... perhaps a love relationship, financial freedom ... freedom from that which has come before, a new job or career.

It matters not what you choose to create for yourself.

In the choosing there is freedom, freedom of expression, freedom to create all your heart's desires.

For in the choosing, your Spirit soars above Earthly limitations of time and space.

Give thanks for all that has come before this moment for it has brought you to where you are.

Give thanks for the many blessings about you.

Have faith all is in Divine Order this moment, occurring in Divine Time.

In the realm of Spirit all is made manifest before you in love and light.

How shall you choose to express yourself this day?

Day 174

DAWNING OF EXPANSION
Angel of the Dawn

⤳

Tis thee wee hour just before dawn, before the dawning of all things
new.
That which is before you, do you choose to see that which is near you,
binding your sight to Earthly concerns?
Do you choose to open your eyes seeing past the illusion of lack, of fear,
uncertainty? Pause for a few moments, breathe deeply ... exhale slowly
beloved child for there is no one, nothing to fear.
Choose to see past physical realm limitations.
Choose instead to see with eyes wide open, embracing the unlimited
Realm of Spirit. Choose to see with an open heart, with an open mind.
Be willingly to experience expansion from within, stretching Earthly
realm concepts past what is known to you this moment.
Be willing to greet all your desires with arms wide open.
Expansion is within your grasp.
Grasp all with open palms, an open heart, with arms wide open.
Embrace the dawning of expansion within you.
Go in Peace this day.

PERCEPTIONS REAL OR PERCEIVED
Zahariel

There are many who would see you in shadow and darkness.
There are many who would tempt you from your path of love, light,
peace, joy, harmony and compassion, abundance and prosperity.
It matters not your perceptions be real or perceived.
It matters only you perceive that which is before you with an open heart,
eyes, an open Spirit.
It matters only you step into the light of forgiveness.
It matters only you step into the realm of harmony and joy.
It matters only you release all that no longer serves your highest and best
good.
It matters only you are willing to release all that would attempt to
overshadow all that is before you.
Be willing to see past Earthly realm perceptions.
Be observant of all that surrounds you.
Are you willing to discover the truth?
Are you willing to accept the many blessings continuing to unfold
before your eyes?
All is brought before you to be polished in the light of Source.
Allow you to be bathed in the brightness of love and mercy all your days.

Day 176

CREATE YOUR OWN REALITY
Archangel Uriel

Beloved child how do you see that which is before you?
Do you see limitation?
Do you see lack?
Do you see all bathed in the light and love of the Creator?
Acknowledge that which is made manifest in the physical, keeping your
sight on that which you desire ... peace, harmony, abundance, joy,
prosperity, love, health.
In all things be aware of where you are, keeping your sight on where you
choose to be. Release that which would attempt to keep you in your
place, allowing no room for expansion.
Open yourself to the richness of all things, people, and places bathed in
Divine Love. Choose to see beauty; choose to become all that you are.
Choose to expand beyond the horizon of limitation set forth by others
upon you.
Choose to create your own reality bathed in the light and love of Divine
Source, for there is no greater glory than to shine forth as a beacon of
light for all.
Peace be with you this day and all the days before you.

Day 177

CELEBRATE TRANSFORMATION
Emmanuel

⌇

Transformation appears in many forms on many levels all in the same
moment. Alchemy is transformation from the leaden Ego mind-chatter
which seeks to distract you from your path.
Alchemy is transformation from lead into gold, the Golden Spark of
Divinity within every living creature great and small.
Celebrate your every step along the way.
Celebrate each step along the path which has brought you to this place,
this time.
A tiny seed of faith, trust, a belief in something better, healing your
Inner-Self has brought about transformation within you.
Transformation is freeing yourself to choose, choosing to be a beacon of
light in a sea of shadow and darkness.
Be as a caterpillar; go within transform yourself from the inside out.
How will you choose to celebrate transformation within you this day?

Day 178

GIFT OF CHOICE
Jaoel

⁓✞⁓

This is the day the Creator hath made.
There are many choices before you.
There are many choices behind you.
Each choice is a step along the path before you.
There is always choice; choice to choose how you shall focus your
thoughts, focus your energy, choosing compassion or judgment.
In the choosing all is made whole.
In the choosing all is healed.
In the choosing, all is revealed.
Seek first the Light of Divine Source within, allowing light to radiate
outward from within you.
Be willing to see your own Divine Spark, sharing the gift with yourself
and all who shall cross your path this day and the next.
Choose wisely, for in choosing you choose also for you.
Become a beacon of light and love shinning forth through perceived
shadow and darkness illuminating the path before you.
All is well beloved child, you are loved beyond measure.

ACCEPTANCE
Archangel Zerachiel

~*~

Trust the process before you this day and all days before you.
All is in Divine Order, occurring in Divine Time.
Appearances are perceptions veiled by that which have come before.
Open yourself to all that awaits you with open arms, an open heart and mind; opening your Soul to Source.
Be aware of that which makes its presence known to you.
Be aware of that which attempts to distract you from your path, from your Life Purpose. There are many choices before you, how do you choose wisely?
Discernment is thy key to all that lay before you this moment.
Breathe deeply the Light of Source, listen, be open to that which is gifted to you.
In stepping forward upon the path before you, know all is in Divine Order, occurring in Divine Time in accordance with your will for your Life Purpose, for your journey in the Earthly realm.
There are no mistakes; things, people, places, experiences simply co-incide one with the other assisting you along the way.
Breathe beloved child, for there is only love and light before you.
There is only love and light which surrounds you.
There is only love and light within you.
Breathe ....

Day 180

LIGHT THE PATH BEFORE YOU
Archangel Remiel

⌒*⌒

Light the path before you with mercy, joy, compassion.
Light the path before you with the light of a thousand golden candles.
In the light there are no shadows or darkness.
In the light there is only that which is for your highest and best good.
In the light there is only love; shadows, real or perceived simply dissolve
into the light. Be willing to receive all that is for your highest and best
good.
As the dawn of a new day approaches, there is choice.
Choice to re-align your energies, your Spirit, thoughts, emotions with all
that is of love and light.
Be not afraid of your own inner desires.
Be not afraid of your Inner-Light.
Be not afraid to be a beacon in the darkness.
Be not afraid of the power within you to dispel all that no longer serves
you.
Be not afraid this day.
Step into the light of Divine Source, love and mercy shall accompany
you all your days.

Day 181

ALL IS WELL
Jeduthun

_✦_

The truth which lies within you speaks volumes for all who would hear
you.
Your Inner-Truth is your outer truth, wear it well.
In the moments of uncertainty, doubt, confusion call upon me.
I shall illuminate the way before you with the light of a thousand
candles.
Light shines in all places, in all people, in all ways, in all directions of
time and space. Give thanks for the many blessings in your life now, this
moment.
Give thanks for that which has brought you to where you are.
Give thanks for all that is before you.
All is well.

Day 182

BE UNAFRAID
Archangel Chamuel

⟳

In seeking Source, you seek yourself.
In the moment of the asking, all is forgiven you.
In the moment of the asking, all is made manifest before you.
In the asking, in the seeking, in the opening, all is revealed.
Do you seek love?
Do you love you wholly and completely?
Do you accept you wholly and completely?
Seek first within, the love of Divine Source.
Be unafraid to remove the mask you show others around you, seeing
past all that has come before for it has no hold upon you.
Be unafraid to step forth on the path before you, for it offers you all your
desires.
Seek first the Realm of Spirit through Divine Source.
Seek first through Source, for Divine Source holds dominion over all
things great and small.
Seek first the light and love within you.
All shall be laid to rest at your feet.
Seek first that which is within you in all ways, in all things.

Day 183

CELEBRATE THE DIVINE IN ALL THINGS
Angel of Glory

In all things, seek first the light within, for it shines before you
illuminating all things, people, places, experiences.
In the light there is only love, peace and harmony, gratitude and
thanksgiving.
In the light there is celebration for countless blessings, tidings of
happiness and joy. Raise your voice to the Heavens, praise Divine Source
for the untold blessings laid at your feet for the asking, in receiving, in
the giving.
All you seek, all you ask ... all is given in the moment of the asking.
How do you prepare yourself for the receiving of your heart's desires?
Do you give thanks for gifts given?
Do you close your eyes to all offered you?
Do you see only that which has come before?
Choose to celebrate the Divine in all things, all faces, in all places ... in
all you will experience from this moment forward.
Choose to celebrate this day and all the days before you.

Day 184

SEEK AND YOU WILL BE FOUND
Archangel Chamuel

He who seeks the love of Divine Source, seeks peace.
He who seeks the light of Divine Source shall be a beacon in the darkness.
He who seeks love and light shall know he Inner-Self.
He who seeks shall be found in the light, wrapped with silvery wings of contentment.
He who seeks inner peace, shall be peaceful all thy days. For in seeking peace, love, light and joy, these things and more shall manifest before you.
All things great and small are manifested in love or fear, light or darkness, peacefulness or chaos.
Seek and you will be found.
Step lightly upon the path before you this day and all your days.

Day 185

PATH LESS TRAVELED
Angel of Serenity

Challenges, conflicts arise before you in many ways presenting illusions
of discontent, mis-trust, dis-ease, dis-harmony.
The path less traveled is one of serenity, releasing that which attempts to
distract you from your true path.
Stay the course beloved child for there is much for you to do, much light
to share amongst all who would see it.
Be not afraid for there is nothing, no one, no experience to fear.
That which at first appears to be an obstacle, a challenge, a loss may
indeed be a blessing gifted to you.
Allow all that is gifted in love and light to seek you.
Allow all that is placed before you that is not of love and light to simply
flow past you for there is no truth in darkness and shadow.
The path less traveled is the way of serenity, peace and joy, harmony and
contentment, abundance and prosperity, a knowing all is well this
moment and every moment. Breathe beloved child for all shall be
revealed.

Day 186

DISCERNMENT
Angel of Discernment

⁓✍⁓

This day as every day there are many choices before you.
In the seeking, in the asking, in the stepping forth along the path before
you, there are many choices.
How do you know which choice is for your highest and best good?
How do you know the difference between that which is your truth and
that which attempts to distract you from your truth?
Take a few moments to breathe deeply of Divine Light.
Feel the Light of Source infill every cell of your physical body.
Breathe deeply exhaling all that does not serve you.
The Light of Divine Source radiates outward from within to all your
energy bodies, gently caressing your entire being.
All things are as they are to be in this moment in perfect union.
Choose emotions, thoughts, actions which serve you and your brethren,
for in choosing the path less traveled, you choose between love and fear,
between light and shadow. Choose wisely, for in the choosing all is made
manifest before you.
As you think, so shall it be.
As you feel, so shall it be.
As you speak, so shall it be.
And so it is.

FLAME OF DIVINITY
Guardian Angel of Spiritual Growth

The flame burns brightly within you, casting out doubt, casting out shadow.
The Spark of Divinity resides within your core essence.
The Spark of Divinity shines forth illuminating all before you.
There are many paths before you.
Choose that which is for you highest and best good.
Choose that which brings peace and harmony, joy, abundance and prosperity, kindness and compassion for you and those around you.
Release that which is before you.
Open your heart, your mind, your Soul.
Release that which is before you knowing all is healed in the moment of the asking. Having asked for healing, step out of your own way; allowing grace to infill you with peaceful contentment.
In the moment of the releasing, the Light of Divine Source shall infill you with loving kindness, compassion.
Step into the light beloved child releasing seeds from days gone by.
Be willing to plant new seeds of faith, trust, love and light in your own inner garden. Tend your garden well, for all blossoms in the light, warmed by the flame of illumination.

Day 188

GIFT OF SERENITY
Angel of Serenity

୰

Serenity is a state of mind, a state of emotion, a state of being.
In all ways, on all levels, serenity is the gift of total surrender of all that
causes struggle, tension, stress, concern or worry.
Serenity is the space between breathes.
Serenity is the space between thoughts.
Serenity is *knowing* all is in Divine Order, occurring in Divine Time
along the path before you.
Serenity is experiencing, even for a brief moment, your eternal
connection to your Higher Self, to Divine Source.
Gift you this day; peace and harmony shall accompany you all your days.

Day 189

PEACEFUL TRANSFORMATION
Archangel Metatron

⌒✳⌒

In all things, in all places, in all people see grace within.
Seek grace within you.
Grace is a state of being, a sense of self, an attitude.
Grace allows you peaceful transformation from what was to what is.
In the Realm of Spirit, grace resides openly and freely for the giving and
the receiving. In the Realm of Spirit all creatures great and small journey
peacefully.
Peaceful transformation is accepting where you are, allowing expansion
within as you travel the path before you to where you want to be.
In all things, in all ways, on all levels gift you with peacefulness.
For in peacefulness, you shall find your way with grace and ease.
Be at peace this day.

Day 190

KNOW THY TRUE SELF
Archangel Gabriel

For all the world, know you beloved Child.
For all the moments which have come before, know you.
For all the moments yet to be, know you.
Do you seek the presence of the I AM within?
That which is like unto itself shall be drawn to you.
Do you speak with love in your heart, mind, voice, Spirit?
If you choose to speak of things not of love, how do you expect to be
loving to yourself and to others?
Love yourself as you would love others.
Love others as you would love yourself.
Speak your truth to you.
Light and Love shall radiate from the I AM presence within.
In all things be truthful.
In all ways be truthful.
You do not need to shout from the mountain tops or through the lush
valleys; Divine Love shall find its own way to sow seeds of Light within
all creatures great and small. Seek first the Light of Divine Source
within; all shall be made bright before you.
Become a beacon for you; illuminate the path before you this day.
Know you.

Day 191

LIGHT AND LOVE
Archangel Zadkiel

To yourself be true.
Know yourself before attempting to know others.
Give to yourself before giving to others.
Heal yourself before attempting to heal others.
Accept yourself before accepting others.
You cannot give to others that which you are unwilling to give to you.
Love you openly, for in truth the love within you radiates from your
inner core essence as a beacon to all who seek a better way.
Be aware of those around you who seek your energy for their own gain.
Be aware of those who seek to distract you from your path.
We ask you acknowledge that which is before you, choosing instead to
step into the Light.
Be strong for the light is challenged in many ways.
Be strong for there are legions of my brethren at the ready to assist in the
moment of the asking.
Be not afraid for the Light and the Love Divine Source and that of my
brethren and me, shall sustain you all your days.
Go in peace this day and all the days yet to be.

Day 192

HARMONY WITHIN
Archangel Raphael

Harmony is a state of mind, emotion.
Harmonious thoughts create a harmonious state of mind, healing body, mind, Soul, and Spirit.
Harmony is a sense of balance in all things, all thoughts, in all emotions.
Harmony is a sense of peacefulness radiating from within your core essence.
Your core essence is untouched by humankind.
Think back for a moment; think back to a time when you felt peaceful, your entire being releasing all that no longer served your highest and best good.
Step into the light before you with love in your heart, mind, in all your energy bodies. Close your eyes but for a moment, for a moment is all that is needed to transport you to that space and time where you were at total peace with all around you.
In truth, that sense of peacefulness is always with you.
In truth you are always in a state of harmonious bliss.
Filter out that which attempts to distract you from your true self.
Know all is well, all is healed.
Seek harmony within.
Harmony shall accompany you all your days.

TRUST FAITH
Ohrmazd

The answer to all things lies within.
Breathe deeply for there is much to celebrate.
Breathe deeply for there is much abundance all around you.
What answers do you seek this day?
In the asking, have you prepared you to receive?
Do you seek strength, patience, health, abundance, harmony?
All these things and more are yours in the moment of the asking.
In truth, that which appears to be an obstacle in this moment may bring
untold riches. Allow your thoughts to be consumed with love and light,
patience, faith and trust that all is in Divine Order.
Allow your thoughts to carry your deepest desires to me and my
brethren, for we await your bidding.
What do you seek this day?
Ask and it is given without delay.

Day 194

PURITY OF WHITE LIGHT
Hashmal

ᴄᴍᴏ

Miracles are the answering of prayer, the seeking of knowledge, the
mending of body, mind and Soul.
Spirit energy within you is Divine, bright white light, unconditional
love.
That, which is bathed in the purity of bright, white light, shines the way
before you. There is nothing that cannot be healed with love.
There is nothing which cannot be healed in the light.
There is nothing which remains in the shadows, for all shall be revealed
in the Light of Divine Source.
Light sustains you.
Light illumines all.
Love is the nectar which surrounds the seen and unseen.
Love is the nectar of life.
Be not afraid to shine forth, casting no shadow about you, giving and
receiving love effortlessly.
As you gift others with grace light, you gift yourself with grace light.
Go within; breathe deeply the purity of white light for it shall
accompany you.

Day 195

DIVINE DIRECTION
Archangel Jehudiel

⌒*⌒

Energy swirls around you in great gusts, gently caressing your skin,
nudging you ever so slightly or carrying you forward by leaps and
bounds.
It matters not how, when, or the speed with which you journey along
your path.
Know there will be pebbles and branches to tug at your feet, thoughts,
emotions, circumstances which create that which appear to be detours.
Detours are opportunities to slow down, breathe, adjust, communicate,
reach out; purge inner stresses.
Many are the challenges in the physical realm.
Challenges are ever present, harmony is ever present.
In those instances, as you find yourself in the midst of seeming chaos,
reach through all that would direct you away from your Divine
Direction of love and light.
Beloved child all is well this day.
All is in Divine Order.
All is occurring in Divine Perfection.
Light a candle of deep indigo blue; imagine all your cares, all your
worries, all that is not of love and light, to be consumed by the light of
the flame.
Know the only truth is love, peace, harmony, bliss, abundance and
prosperity. Journey towards the light, be steady, all is well this day.

Day 196

CYCLES
Archangel Sariel

Breathe deeply beloved child for Source Light shall guide you all the days before you. Breathe deeply; giving thanks for all that has come before.

Breathe deeply giving thanks, opening you to all that is yet to come.

Breathe deeply, acknowledge where you are in this moment, giving thanks for all that is yet to be.

The shimmering light of the moon is a symbol of the never-ending cycle of unity and Oneness with Divine Source Energy.

As with all things great and small, there are cycles; cycles of awakening, cycles of sleeping, cycles of joy, cycles of planting, reaping the fruits of your labors.

It matters not which cycle you are experiencing this moment, for all shall come full circle manifesting in physical form as it is in the Realm of Spirit.

Day 197

DISINTEGRATE DIRTY ENERGY
Angels of the Violet Flame

⌒⋙⌒

We, Angels of the Violet Flame surround you in the most beautiful violet light. Close your eyes, breathe deeply, exhale all worries, concerns, releasing all stresses this day, surrounding you with violet light.
Feel, sense, see, brilliant violet light all round your physical body extending beyond all your energy bodies.
Violet light is above you, behind you, in front of you, below you.
Dare to see the brilliant white-hot flames of violet light disintegrate all dirty, negative energy within and around you.
Trust this is so.
Trust in your Self-Power, ask us to assist you, we are many, we are everywhere every moment.
Allow Angels of the Violet Flame to surround you, protect you, to keep you safe from harmful thoughts, emotions, energies, circumstances of others.
Now, this moment all is that is not for your highest and best good, all that is not of love and light, all thoughts, emotions, circumstances, situations, experiences, *all* that is not of love and light, now, this moment disintegrates.
Violet light protection surrounds you in the moment of the asking.
You need only think the words Violet Light … it is done.
Violet Light shall make the way before you clear, burning away all that is not of love and light.
Trust this is so … so be it, so be it, so be it thank you.

Day 198

SURRENDER
Archangel Uriel

⟶⟋⟍

Allow ideas, thoughts, choices to flow freely.
Do not become obsessive about that which you desire.
Do allow that which you desire to come into your life with ease and grace.
Follow your inner guidance, releasing the need to have all, do all, to know all in a single moment.
Breathe in ... exhaling slowly ... breathe deeply. Calm yourself with each breath, exhaling slowly.
Ask me and my brethren to assist you in surrendering all that would attempt to distract you from a state of peace, harmony, and joy.
In the wake of releasing all that no longer serves you, open yourself to all that awaits you in the Realm of Spirit.
In the eyes of Divine Source, all is made manifest in the asking, the seeking.
Surrender any fears, thoughts of lack, limitation.
Know all is given to you, for there is no purpose in keeping you from your good.
Open yourself to all which lay at your feet.
Know all is in Divine Order.
You cannot see the whole of the journey in an instant; the journey unfolds as a tapestry is created one stitch at a time.
Each breath, each step is an opportunity to choose differently.
How shall you choose this day?

Day 199

UNCONDITIONAL RELEASE
Gadiel

Release that which causes dis-harmony.
Release that which is conditional.
Release that which does not serve your highest and best good.
Release all that is not of love and light.
Call upon me to clear the path before you, lighting each step upon your path in brilliant white light.
There is no place, no space for any shadow thought, emotion, circumstance, or situation to conceal itself.
There is only love. There is only light.
In the beginning all was made in the likeness of Spirit, Divine Source.
All is made in love. All is made in light.
Imagine a balloon, a beautiful emerald green balloon ... breathe deeply
... exhale slowly filling the balloon with all thoughts of lack, situations, which cause dis-comfort, dis-harmony.
Breathe in light ... exhale all shadow and darkness into the balloon.
Breathe deeply, inhaling the Divine Light ... exhale shadow.
Tie a beautiful, bright yellow, silken ribbon to seal *all* inside the balloon.
In love and light, release the balloon. The balloon begins to rise above all Earthly concerns. The balloon rises higher, higher, higher still.
The balloon continues to rise, you feel lighter and lighter.
The balloon has risen so high, it has become a tiny speck.
You no longer see the balloon; there is no thing, person, situation, nor circumstance to hold you from your good.
Allow yourself to be free. All is well.

Day 200

INNER PEACE, INNER HARMONY
Archangel Raziel

∽ﮡ∾

All is given for nothing is ever kept from you.
What do you seek?
Who do you seek?
Do you seek to know your Inner-Spirit?
Do you seek inner peace, health, prosperity, harmony, love?
How shall you know these things and more if first you do not seek all
within you?
Do not look to others to provide that which you seek.
Do seek others who are like minded to guide and assist you along the
path before you. Do reach out with loving-kindness to all who seek the
light and love of Divine Source. Take care lest you cast upon others your
inner fears of lack.
Nurture Divine Light within you with love, compassion, joy,
peacefulness.
Take care beloved child, accept that which is, keeping your eyes open to
all that is yet to be.
All shall be revealed in the light, in reality there is no darkness.
Release you and others from all that has come before this moment.
This moment is all there is.
Go in peace this day; peace shall accompany you all your days.

Day 201

PATIENT MANIFESTATION
Theliel

⌒*⌒

Patience is vital in manifesting all you desire.
Patience is stepping softly, slowly seeing beauty all around you.
Seeing, hearing, feeling, speaking with love creates a peaceful, harmonious energy in and around you.
Your inner light shines more brightly, attracting to you all that you desire.
What do you seek?
What do you desire?
In discovering what you do not want, you discover that which you desire.
Focus your thoughts, emotions, energy on your desires, planting the seeds of your desires with love; tending your inner garden with humility, compassion, and patience. Be willing to commit your entire being to all you desire.
Be open to receiving all your requests.
Be willing to practice patience during the time of transition between the planting of the seeds and the harvest of your desires.
Be willing to celebrate all the steps along the path before you as your heart's desires are made manifest.
Patience beloved one, for all is occurring in Divine Time.
Patience, for all shall be revealed to you.
Patience ....

Day 202

UNCONDITIONAL LOVE
Hadraniel

∼∼∼

Begin again, dream larger, dream clearer.
Breathe deeply beloved one for all things begin again with clarity,
patience, healing, harmony, joy, peace.
A slight breeze brushes your skin, gently clearing away all pain and
sorrow.
There is only unconditional love, there is only eternal light.
Promises of man to man, in the moment of the making, are real,
unconditional.
Keep faith strong. Keep your heart open.
Allow the storm to rage, purging all inside you.
Allow Divine Light, the light of Angelic Choirs to illuminate your
entire being.
Shadow has no place to hide. All shall be revealed in the light.
All shall be released in the light. All shall be given to you in the light.
All is given you unconditionally; ask for it is given in the moment of the
asking.
The question remains, are you open to receive all you ask in the moment
of the asking? Limitation is a state of mind. Limitation is of your
making.
Limitation is allowing the perception of loss, fear, lack to block the light
and love of the Divine Source.
Unconditional love cannot be contained for it is eternal, always shining
before you, illuminating the path before you.
Beloved one, open the gates within you now this moment.
Fear not, for you shall step upon stones of gold or be taught to fly.

Day 203

GIFT OF TRANSFORMATION
Emmanuel

Transformation is the gateway to freedom; freedom from all which
attempts to distract you from your path.
Transformation is freedom from all that has come before this moment.
Transformation is freedom from pain and sorrow, real or perceived.
Transformation is freedom from thoughts of limitation or lack.
Imagine a butterfly fluttering nearby.
The butterfly was once a caterpillar, having transformed itself into a
beautiful winged creature!
Transformation is the seeking of light, seeking of love ... love for you, as
you are whole, complete and perfect now this moment.
Transformation is a gift of shedding old ways of thinking, feeling,
traveling along the path before you.
Transformation is being open to receive the gifts which await you in the
Realm of Spirit. Transformation is a gift to be treasured.
How shall you celebrate your transformation this day?

Day 204

BALANCE, RE-BALANCE
Camel

∽᷎∾

In all things seek balance.
In work and play seek balance.
In action and solitude seek balance.
There are many choices before you this day; choice between light and
shadow, love and anger, dis-harmony and harmony, despair and joy,
suffering and healing.
Each step, each breath, each thought gifts you with choice, to choose
differently than the moment before.
Gift yourself with a moment of silence, re-balancing thoughts,
emotions, action or non-action.
Light a green candle, focus upon the flame.
The flame of a candle is steady, burning brightly, a beacon of light in the
darkness.
At times there is movement, enough movement to snuff the light of the
candle, simply re-light the flame ... re-light the flame within you.
That which is before you, seek the nugget of joy within the situation or
circumstance; seek balance in thought, emotion, action.
Seek peace within, seek the light, seek harmony.
Seek balance this day and the days before you.
Go in peace.

Day 205

SPIRIT WITHIN
Guardian Angel of the Inner Child

In the beginning all was made in the likeness of the Creator.
In the beginning all creatures great and small knew of the Creator's love,
mighty, pure white light of unconditional love.
In days long since past, many seek the light, nurturing, acceptance,
unconditional love. That which you do not accept within, cannot be
obtained from sources outside of you. Every breath, every step along the
path before you is a gift of renewed hope, healing, acceptance,
innocence.
Call upon me to protect, nurture all new beginnings ... new career
choices, new relationships with yourself and that of another.
Release all sorrow, emotional and physical pain.
Cherish the Spark of Divinity within.
Cherish all that is of love and light. Cherish all thy heartfelt desires.
Cherish your inner child, cradle hopes, dreams, aspirations with
unconditional acceptance, unconditional love.
Surround your inner child with the purity of the Creator's light and love.
Allow you to remain open to all that is before you.
Be aware of that which tempts to distract you.
Be aware of people, circumstances which would harm you.
Remain open beloved one for in your openness all is seen, all is revealed,
all is given, all is received in love and light.
Shed only tears of healing and happiness.
Step from the shadows into the light, honoring your Inner-Spirit.
Cherish these steps as if they are your first, for in reality, these are your
first steps into blissful harmony and joy, peace and tranquility, love and
light.

Day 206

IN THE FACE OF ADVERSITY
Domiel

When all about you are fearful, breathe deeply of indigo light.
Feel or sense indigo light gently weave through your entire being,
physical and ethereal. Feel a sense of calm peacefulness with each breath
... exhale all your worries and concerns.
Breathe deeply, allowing indigo light to weave its magic within.
Exhale slowly releasing all you wish to release to the Heavens and into
the light for transmutation.
Begin to see beauty all around you, open your eyes to the many
blessings, gifts given for all is healed, all is forgiven, all is given you this
day and all the days before you.
Be joyous; appreciate the divinity within, radiate love and peace,
harmony and joy. When all about you are fearful, smile for you carry the
light and love of the Creator within.
Go in peace, walk in the light.

Day 207

SACRED FLAME
Nathaniel

⚜

Beloved one, seek first the light of the Divine Source within.
Cleanse, purify your thoughts, emotions, your entire physical body.
Allow the Flame of Source to release you from all worries, concerns,
stresses, hurts and sorrows.
The Sacred Flame within grows stronger with each breath, each healing,
each release. Open to all that is holy within.
Open yourself to all that is of love and light.
Open to giving of love and light to you and to others.
Open to receive all that is already yours in the Realm of Spirit.
Allow that which is already made manifest in the Realm of Spirit to be
made manifest in the physical realm.
All is laid at your feet.
How shall you choose to walk upon the path laid before you?
Shed the skin of what was; clothe yourself with radiant light and love.
Gift you with loving thoughts, loving actions.
Create for you a new skin, radiating light from your inner core essence
of pure unconditional love.

Day 208

BEGIN AGAIN
Gazardiel

～*ff*～

Begin again.
Begin again to express yourself with loving kindness.
Begin again with each breath.
Begin again with the rising of the sun.
Allow all that has come before to fade as day flows from dusk to night.
The rising of the moon in its fullness soon gives way to begin again,
renewing the cycle of life.
Rise to greet the sun as it begins its journey across the Heavens.
Breathe in Divine Light.
Breathe in light, exhale shadow and darkness for all is revealed in the
light.
The path before you welcomes you this day and all the days before you.
Close your eyes; imagine bright red-oranges, deep golden yellows.
Perhaps you see deep rose pinks or turquoise blues.
Rest a moment in the stillness, allowing peacefulness, joy and harmony
to be your constant companions.

Day 209

ARE YOU WILLING?
Archangel Raphael

～*w*～

What do you seek this day?
Call upon me to guide your journey inward.
Call upon me when seeking clarity of mind, clarity of Spirit.
Call upon me to guide your footsteps upon the path before you.
Call upon me beloved child, for all is healed in the moment of the
asking.
All is healed in the moment of belief.
All is healed; all is forgiven you this moment.
Are you willing to release limiting thoughts, beliefs, past hurts real or
perceived?
Are you willing to forgive yourself and others for wrongs done by you or
to you?
Are you willing to see past what once was?
Are you willing to see beyond physical realm limitations?
Are you willing to see the Christ Light within all creatures great and
small, including you?
Are you willing to release yourself into your greater good, remaining
open to receive gifts given you?
Are you willing .....

Day 210

VISION OF SEEING
Haziel

⌒ᵐ⌒

As you look around, what do you see?
Do you see limitation or limitlessness, dis-ease or health, lack or
abundance?
Do you see dis-harmony or harmony?
Do you see chaos or peacefulness in your surroundings?
There is much before you this moment; choose to see past physical
realm perceptions of fear and lack, distrust of your fellow human kind.
Choose instead to be aware of that which is before you; choose to
acknowledge that which is a truth for another without creating their
truth as your own.
Truth is that which resonates within you.
Choose to see past physical real limitations of others, their truth need
not be your truth. You are free to choose, seeing through the eyes of my
brethren and me and that of Divine Source.
Vision is seeing through eyes of love and compassion.
Are you willing to see you through eyes of love and compassion as
Source sees you?
Are you willing to see all creatures great and small with love and
compassion? Vision ... Vision ... how shall you choose to see this day?

Day 211

DEGREES OF TRANSFORMATION
Ezekiel

⌒⌒

Transforming thoughts, emotions, actions, is as simple or as complicated
as you choose. Easy is a word to measure degrees of difficulty or
challenge one faces as choices present themselves for consideration.
Allow you to feel, acknowledging where you are keeping your heart and
mind on where you want to be, do or have.
Seeking Divine Light is as simple as stepping out from shadow and
darkness into the light.
Stepping into Divine Light is as simple as stepping to the side, allowing
the shadows of others to flow past you.
Transformation is pivoting from one point of view to another in one
leap or one step at a time along the path before you.
Sound the trumpet!
Allow only light and love into your heart, mind, into your Soul.
Sound the trumpet!
Allow the wind to move all that no longer serves your highest and best
good from you. Sound the trumpet!
Allow the rain to wash from you sorrow and pain.
Sound the trumpet!
All is forgiven, all is made whole, all is made complete.
You are whole, complete and perfect, now this moment.
Travel in peaceful harmony this day beloved one, for you are loved
beyond measure.

Day 212

FLAME OF TRANSFORMATION
Malkhiel

Look to the Heavens for inspiration in all things no matter the size, the
importance, the complexity.
Look to the Heavens, for the Heavens symbolize the power within you
to rise above, flow in and around that which is before you this moment.
All challenges present you with an opportunity to accept the Flame of
Transformation being gifted to you.
All challenges present you with an opportunity to rise above, much as
smoke rises above the fire.
If at times you feel the need to rest a moment as you journey along the
path before you, breathe in light and unconditional love given for the
asking by Source.
Gift yourself with rest, taking a few moments to look about you,
observing where you have been, where you are and where you desire to
be.
Acknowledge all that has come before.
Give thanks for lessons learned, people, places and things encountered
along the way. Accept you in all your glory for you are a child of the
cosmos, Divine Source within all living things.
Ignite the spark within you, rise above, look to the Heavens, look within
for all things are possible in the light.

Day 213

BEFRIEND YOU
Raguel

⟶

Befriend you.
Be in integrity with yourself.
Be just with you.
Be gentle with you.
Be compassionate with you.
Be that which you desire in another.
Be not afraid to acknowledge your true Self, your inner core essence.
We do not ask you go about exposing your core essence.
We ask you accept your core essence, your radiant Inner-Self.
Accepting you is to embrace all that has come before bringing you to this moment. Accepting you, is acknowledging where you find yourself now this moment.
Accepting you, is being open to all you desire, knowing there are no limitations, no lack, no fear, only love and light illuminating the path before you.
Befriend you.
Call upon me and my brethren, we shall open the way before you this day and all the days yet to come.

Day 214

UNCONDITIONAL TRUST
Asariel

⁓

Trust is the key to thy very expansion; expansion in Spirit; expansion in your heart center; expansion in your awareness; expansion in all relationships; expansion in accepting your true Self, your inner core essence.

You may ask how is that possible, to trust unconditionally?

Discernment is the key unlocking a magical journey before you.

Trust is a gift freely given. Trust is first given to you.

Do you trust your intuition, messages given you? Do you trust your own judgment?

In whom do you place your deepest sense of trust? Trust you.

As there are layers of soil covering Mother Earth, there are layers of trust. There are many who are trustworthy. There are many in whom you confide.

There are few you entrust with your life. There are fewer still you in whom you trust your innermost feelings, your deepest desires, your fears.

Expressing unconditional trust is an exercise is discernment, faith in the unseen.

Trust is knowing when and in whom to open yourself completely.

Trust your sense of knowing, trust you sense of sight, trust your sense of hearing, trust your entire being.

Should there be doubt, wait, for there is good reason. Your Core Essence, your true Self is a most sacred gift.

Gift yourself with trust wholly and completely, without reservation, accepting that which is thy truth.

The truth of others does not serve you unconditionally; accept you with an open heart, mind, an open Soul unconditionally.
You cannot first trust others and then trust you.
You must first trust you unconditionally all else flows freely for the asking, for the giving.

Day 215

CHOOSE YOUR POINT OF FOCUS
Charmeine

In the early dawn of the morn all rise with the glorious light of the sun; a symbol of light, warmth, of passions renewed.
Think back, for a moment, to that which has passed.
Were there not moments, many moments of joy, happiness, laughter, love?
Perhaps there was but a moment or two that were not as you wanted them to be.
Will you choose to dwell in this place?
Choose instead to dwell in those moments which brought joy, laughter, happiness, hope and faith in the moments yet to be.
Choose to dwell among thoughts, feelings of joy, love and happiness.
You will attract to you more joy, happiness, laughter, and love.
Choosing to dwell on the few moments of fleeting disappointment and you will attract to you more disappointment.
Choose your point of focus wisely.

DIVINE TRUTH
Zagzagel

Truth lay in the wisdom and knowledge of the ages.
If this were so, how then would you go about seeking the keys to
unlocking the great secrets of this ancient wisdom and knowledge?
Look to you, go within, seek the silence in between thoughts, between
breaths.
Look you, all you seek lay within you.
Thoughts, emotions, actions contain nuggets of your Golden Truth.
Gold is purity of thought, emotional purity, and purity of intention.
Gold is the covering of protection.
Your inner core essence is smelted, heated and purified, transforming
leaden energy into Golden Light.
Light a candle of gold, focus for a few moments on the flame.
What colors do you see within the flame?
Imagine all that would cause you worry or pain to be consumed in the
flame of the candle.
All is transformed into pure, radiant light, released to the Heavens for
healing.
Truth lay in the wisdom and knowledge of the ages.

Day 217

CREATE THIS DAY
Archangel Uriel

⌇

Create this day as you wish it to be.
Create thoughts, emotions, actions which resonate with your inner truth.
Create your life as you desire it to be.
Do you desire better health?
Do you desire harmonious relationships?
Do you desire greater financial freedom, abundance and prosperity?
Do you desire a love relationship?
All these things and more are yours for the asking.
You need only express gratitude for all being as you desire it or better.
You need only be open to receiving all you desire.
You need only give thanks; all is given to you in the moment of the asking.
There is nothing denied you except through your own dis-belief, non-acceptance, thoughts of un-worthiness.
Light a candle of white, allow the flame to illuminate the path before you this day.
All is revealed in the Light.
All is given and received in love.
Open your heart and mind to all that are creating this day.

MOMENTS OF REMEMBERING
Archangel Chamuel

There are many situations, people, thoughts, emotions before you this moment.
Perhaps some of what is before you is in part, what is also behind you.
It is important to remember that which has brought you to where you are.
It is not so important to recall all details of what is now behind you.
In those moments of remembering, allow the thought or emotion to rise, allow it to continue to rise in love, into Source Light.
All is given to you, all is forgiven you.
Do you in turn give forgiveness to yourself?
The path before you is clear and bright, filled with love, joy, happiness, peace, patience, tolerance, acceptance, abundance and prosperity, health and healing.
Seek first the light and love of Divine Source and you shall find you.
The journey before you is filled awe and wonder.
Travel the path before you with gentleness and understanding knowing all is in Divine Order for you this day and all the days before you.

Day 219

STEP INTO THE LIGHT
Mithra

Seeking Divine Light is more than coming from shadow into light.
In seeking Divine Light, you are in essence speaking to your Inner-Self,
expressing a desire to see, to be heard, to feel, to heal.
Seeking Divine Light is seeking your core essence; you are whole and
complete now this moment.
There is no other like you.
In the light, there are no secrets, all is revealed for the asking.
In the light, there is no place for fear there is only love.
In the light, there is no lack there is only abundance.
In the light there, there is no darkness all is illuminated.
Step into the light beloved one, you are a gift to yourself and those
around you.
Step into the light; release all your burdens.
Step into the light; shed all that no longer serves you.
Step into the light.

Day 220

EXPRESS YOUR TRUTH
Jeduthun

Sing, speak, write. It matters not the way in which you express your truth.

What is your truth?

Are you willing to go within, sitting in the silence, hushing the small voice which chatters in your head all the day?

Are you willing to draw back the veil between your inner core essence and that which you show others?

Are you willing to choose in whom you confide your innermost yearnings?

Are you willing to peel away the mask you wear in the comfort and safety of your home? Are you willing to be open to that which you seek?

Are you willing to give of yourself, to release all that no longer serves your highest and best interests?

Are you willing to forsake all others, the truths of others, the desires others would have for you?

You are a child of light, an expression of unconditional love, non-judgment, a singer of songs.

You are whole and complete now this moment.

How shall you choose to express your truth this day?

Day 221

EXPRESS JOY, KINDNESS, LAUGHTER
Asaliah

⟶

Your ways are to be just.
Your ways are the ways of the Creator.
Look around you, what do you see?
What do you feel?
What do you hear?
Do you judge yourself and others harshly?
Do you accept yourself as you accept others?
Do you accept others as you accept yourself?
Are you willing to look within this day and all the days before you?
Are you willing to see another's point of view?
We do not ask you take another's point of view as your own.
We ask you consider seeing without filters, expressing loving kindness.
Speak with truth and integrity.
Speak with love and light.
See healing and health.
See prosperity and abundance.
Feel harmony and peace.
Express joy and laughter.
Radiate love, step into Divine Light this day, all your days shall be filled
with awe.

Day 222

TRANSITION, EXPANSION, AWARENESS
Archangel Sariel

⌒✎⌒

In all things, in all people, in all places, know you and all shall flow
peacefully, harmoniously into place within and around you.
Look to me and my brethren for protection, guidance, healing,
harmony, knowledge.
In the seeking you will find.
In the asking you will receive.
In the knocking upon the door, all shall be opened to you.
Each moment, each breath, each step forward along the path before you
is an opportunity to go beyond what is known.
Be not afraid beloved one for you are loved, you are guided beyond
measure.
Seek answers first within.
Each breath gifts you with another.
Each moment of peacefulness gifts you with another.
Each moment of joy gifts you with another.
Each moment of gratitude and appreciation gifts you with more to be
thankful for, appreciating many blessings.
What do you seek?
For what do you yearn?
In all things, in all people, in all places seek peace; harmony shall
accompany you all your days and nights.

Day 223

EMERGE IN WHOLENESS
Radueriel

✽

Do you seek the wisdom of the ages or perhaps the wisdom you seek is discernment, aligning yourself with Divine Source and that of Universal Knowledge.
How shall you go about seeking this wisdom, the wisdom of discernment?
Sit in the silence, sing songs of praise and gratitude, give unconditionally to you.
Perhaps you prefer to write; express yourself in ways which resonates within. Discernment creates a sense of knowing within, a knowing that all is well, all is occurring in Divine Time in accordance with the Divine Plan for your life.
We do not say all is pre-destined for there are as many choices as there are birds, bees and butterflies.
Winged creatures take flight easily and effortlessly ... so too can you.
Take flight beloved one for there are many choices all gently guiding your footsteps along the path before you.
Take heed; listen to the still small voice within, for it is the Divine Spark of Divinity within, speaking your truth of love and light.
Create the life you desire. Transmute negative energy within you.
Emerge in wholeness. Discernment provides choice.
Discernment provides the wisdom to know that which is for your highest and best good. Insight is knowing, knowing all is as it is to be.
Insight is knowing your truth.
Insight is knowing what has come before may no longer resonate within you. Insight is trusting all is well this day.

Day 224

PEACEFUL CONTENTMENT
Remiel

⌒*⌒

All you seek is within you this moment.

All you have asked for is within you this moment.

It is easy to say all is in Divine Order, occurring in Divine Time for your highest and best good.

The challenge in the physical realm lay in not knowing when or how all shall come to pass.

We ask for your patience; allow my brethren and me to guide you, illuminating the path before you with Divine White Light.

Allow your Self to accept there are others involved in your desires.

Allow you to know, trust and have faith all is well with you this day.

Allow your Inner-Self to become still, filled with peaceful contentment as all is made manifest before you.

We are not asking you to surrender your hopes, your dreams, your heart's desires. Instead we ask you release into our hands the how, the when of things yet to be.

We ask you trust your Inner-Self, knowing all is developing better than you envision.

All that you desire may at first appear to be simple and straightforward causing temporary dis-harmony within.

Know; trust there is more to weaving a beautiful tapestry than selecting many colored threads.

Allow you to experience the journey, releasing all that no longer serves you along the way.

Become peaceful, contentment shall bring all your desire's to you without delay.

Day 225

MANY BLESSINGS
Barakiel

～*～

There are many blessings, gifts given you.
In the light of day in the darkness of night, look about you what do you see?
Are you willing to open your eyes, truly seeing all that is given you for the asking?
Ah you say ... there is much I do not desire, how then can these be called blessings?
We ask you this ... go within seek the answers.
Did you ask for what you wanted or simply cling to all that you desire to be rid of?
It is said the focus of your thoughts, your emotions intensifies all within you whether it be to manifest more harmony or dis-cord.
Search within you ... what thoughts; emotions are within your heart, your mind?
If you are not pleased, change your thoughts, your emotions and all about you shall be transformed.
Have faith, trust all is well.

Day 226

BECOME THE CANDLE
Mihr

ᴍ

Each time you meet another upon the path, a relationship begins.
It may come to pass, the relationship lasts but for a moment or longer.
With each meeting of another there is an exchange of energy.
In the blink of an eye all may change.
You may very well be the catalyst for change in another simply having
given a smile.
A smile is the simplest, deepest single gift from you to another.
A touch, a kind word, loving thoughts, a kind gesture may be a most
profound turning point for the receiver.
Give of yourself unconditionally.
Give to yourself unconditionally.
Imagine you are lighting a candle.
Light two more candles from the flame of the first.
Does the light of the first candle become dim in the giving?
No, the first candle shares the flame and the light without hesitation,
there is no sacrifice in the giving.
Become like the candle, sharing the light within you.
Give freely this day.

Day 227

DIVINE JUSTICE
Archangel Zadkiel

Divine Justice is filled with loving integrity.
Divine Justice is unconditional surrender of all that is not of love and light.
Divine Justice is graceful harmony.
Divine Justice is seeking peaceful contentment within.
Divine Justice is stepping into the Light of the Creator, radiating love and light to all regardless of deed, regardless of worthiness.
Divine Justice is simply being in the moment, allowing *all* too simply be.
For in allowing *all* too simply be, you shine forth in the darkness, a beacon of light for all who choose a better way.
Be a beacon for yourself.
Be a beacon for all to see.
All is well this day.

Day 228

STRENGTH IS ...
Uzzah

⌒⁓⌒

Be strong for there are many who would seek your destruction.
Be strong for there are many who seek to extinguish the flame within you.
Be strong for there are many who seek a better way.
Be strong for yourself, for there are distractions, challenges before you.
Strength is knowing when to speak and when to stay quiet.
Strength is knowing the light, the Spark of Divinity within shall always light the way. Strength is knowing, trusting, having faith all is in Divine Order, all is falling into place easily without effort.
Strength is knowing when to stand thy ground and when it to step aside.
Strength is knowing all is made manifest before you without condition, without limitation.
Strength is knowing you are whole, complete and perfect now this moment.
Strength is knowing when to reach out to another.
Strength is knowing when to seek thy own counsel.
Strength is .....

Day 229

CHOOSING FORGIVENESS
Uzziel

∽

All is forgiven in the moment of the asking.
All is forgiven another in the moment of the asking.
All is healed in the moment of gifting yourself with unconditional
forgiveness.
All is healed in the moment of gifting those who cause you pain,
unconditional forgiveness.
Choosing forgiveness does not cause you more harm or place you in
harm's way. Choosing forgiveness releases you from all that has come
before, clearing the way for all that is before you.
In choosing forgiveness, you choose freedom from bondage of all that
no longer serves you or your purpose.
In choosing forgiveness, you chose to see through eyes of love and
beauty.
In choosing forgiveness, you release you from all that would hold from
you all that awaits you.
In choosing forgiveness, you choose love and light.
In choosing forgiveness, you gift another with the choice of releasing
themselves from bondage.
Choose peace.
Choose love.
Choose forgiveness.
Mercy and compassion shall be your constant companions.
The open door that awaits you, have courage, have faith, step forward
into all that awaits you along your path this day.

Day 230

INTEGRITY OF SPIRIT
Ha'amiah

⁓ゆ⁓

Honor yourself. Honor guidance received.
Honor your heart's desires.
Honor choices, paths chosen by others.
It is not the will of Divine Source that you shall direct another.
Direct instead yourself towards the light.
Honor your thoughts, emotions.
Honor your actions ... think before you act.
Your thoughts, your actions affect all who come into contact with you.
This is not to say you must be ever watchful over all words, thoughts,
emotions,
We are asking you to be aware of your inner desires.
Is what you are doing, saying, thinking, feeling resonating with your
Inner-Self?
Are you in integrity with you?
Are you knowingly stepping away from your true Self?
As knowingly stepping away from your true Self, your inner core essence
causes you harm, it causes others harm for you are not acting with
integrity.
Resist temptation, stay in the light.
Ask my brethren and me to wrap you in the light and love of Divine
Source.
Become a guardian for yourself.
Become a beacon, stepping out of the shadows into the light.
Resonate with yourself and all that you are; all shall fall into place as it is
to be.

Day 231

CONTENTMENT
Hadraniel

⌒✼⌒

In the blink of an eye, all things change.
Each breath is an opportunity to release that which is behind you.
Each step along the journey brings possibilities of all things filled with joy, happiness, love, light, prosperity and abundance, peace ... a sense of contentment.
Contentment is being at peace within and with you.
Contentment is expressing appreciation for where you are, now this moment. Contentment is expressing joy and laughter.
Contentment radiates outward into all things, all places, all experiences.
Contentment is appreciating where you are in this moment, keeping your eye on the pot of gold at the end of the Rainbow.
There is much to be thankful for.
There is much you desire to do, experience, give and receive.
Keep your eye on the prize.
Accept where you are, look to where you choose to be ...work with yourself, release the fear of not having, not doing, not being all you desire for yourself.
In the blink of an eye, all things change.
Contentment is graceful acceptance of now.
Contentment is allowing you to move with love, light, and grace along the path before you.
Contentment is.

Day 232

OPEN MIND, OPEN HEART
Barakiel

⌒*⌒

In the name of the Creator, give thanks for there is much too thankful for.
In the name of the Creator, humble yourself to receive all that is made
manifest in the Realm of Spirit in your name.
Doubt not all that awaits you.
Doubt not all your good shall be made manifest in physical form before
you.
Have faith all is arriving in Divine Time.
It may appear thy good is being kept from you. We ask you look about ...
can you not see the many blessings which surround you this moment?
Are you willing to accept that which is, looking to what shall be?
Are you open to receiving your heart's desires?
Do you seek peace and harmony, healing and forgiveness, joy and
laughter?
That which you seek with an open heart, open mind shall be gifted to you.
Know you are loved, cherished, and blessed beyond measure.
Look behind you, have you not journeyed along the path before you
learning, loving, forgiving, healing yourself beyond your imagination?
How then can you doubt? Trust, have faith that all is occurring in
Divine Time.
Give thanks for there is much to be thankful for.
Accept all that is shown to you, for there are untold gifts with each step
along the path. With an open heart, an open mind lovingly set one foot
before the other, the path before you is more beautiful, more loving,
more harmonious, more abundant than you imagine for you are a most
precious gift of love and light.
Go forth beloved one, for you are loved beyond measure.

Day 233

SMILE, ALL AWAITS YOU
Archangel Raziel

～

Rejoice this day! Daybreak brings many blessings, many choices to begin anew.

Breathe in happiness and joy, exhale sadness and disappointment.

Breathe in light and love, exhale shadow and dis-content.

Breathe in limitless possibilities, exhale lack and limitation.

All is before you this moment.

There is nothing you cannot experience.

There is nothing you cannot be.

There is nothing you cannot have.

There is nothing denied you.

Open your heart, open your mind.

Sing a different song, tell a different story. All is laid at your feet. Step into the light beloved one.

Smile at the naysayers for they are poor in Spirit.

Smile at the naysayers for they would have you accompany them in shadow and darkness.

Step into the light, claim all that is truly yours in the Realm of Spirit.

Step into the Light of the Creator, warm your entire being.

Day 234

YOU ARE CALLED UPON
Sapiel

You are called upon each moment to radiate light and love.
You are called upon to speak your truth.
You are called upon to be compassionate.
You are called upon to forgive others for their transgressions against you
and others. You are called upon to forgive yourself in times of doubt and
fear.
You are called upon to love you and others unconditionally.
Unconditional love does not mean you must stay where you no longer
desire to be. Unconditional forgiveness does not mean you must remain
on your current path. Unconditional is without condition.
Light shines upon you without condition.
Light shines through you without condition.
Love is given to you without condition.
Choose to be unconditional.
Choose to be compassionate.
Choose to be love.
Choose to be forgiving.
Choose to see grace where there is none.
Choose wisely.
All that is within you, you radiate outward giving and receive in kind.
You are called upon, how shall you choose to answer?

Day 235

FAITH, TRUST, BELIEF IN THE DIVINE
Sealtiel

⁓ᴍ⁓

Contemplate the path before you this day.
It is not the same as that which lay before you yesterday nor is it the
same path in the light of another dawn.
That which has come before is behind you.
Sorrow, injustice, disappointment all are behind you now this moment.
Look to the light beloved one, all your desires are granted in the
moment of wanting, in the moment of speaking aloud, in the moment
of declaring your heartfelt desires.
It may at first appear as though you are not heard, you desires
overlooked.
Believe not in the absence of that which is yet to be made manifest in
physical form for all is granted without delay, without condition.
Allow yourself to believe, to have faith, to trust all is in Divine Order
occurring in Divine Time.
Yes, we understand it may appear these words are empty, without
substance, just beyond your grasp.
If you will trust, hold firm this or something better, it shall be so this day
and all the days before you.
What shall you request of me brethren and me this day and all the days
before you?

Day 236

ESSENCE OF SERENITY
Angel of Serenity

The essence of serenity is the space between breaths.
The essence of serenity is the shudder of releasing all that attempts to hold you from your good.
The essence of serenity is a smile you gift another.
The essence of serenity is forgiving yourself for accepting even for a moment, the perception of having failed.
The essence of serenity is seeing a rainbow grace the sky, or a full moon casting its brilliant light upon the ground.
The essence of serenity is sharing the silence with kindred spirits, those of like mind. The essence of serenity is focusing upon the flame of the candle, letting all else fall from you.
The essence of serenity is simply being in a state of grace knowing all is in Divine Order occurring in Divine Time.
The essence of serenity is knowing all is well with you this moment and all the moments before you.
Open yourself to all that is before you; allow grace and harmony to gift you with the essence of serenity this day.
All is well beloved one, for you are loved beyond your knowing.

Day 237

PATH OF ACCEPTANCE
Angel of Mercy

Gift yourself with forgiveness, patience, acceptance, laughter and joy.
Gift yourself with love, peace, harmony.
All are gifts of mercy.
All are gifts given without measure, without condition.
How then can you deny you these gifts and more?
How then can you deny the gift of mercy to another?
Perhaps there is someone or something before you that is not to your
liking.
You have a choice of accepting that which is and turn your thoughts to
love and light or cast more shadow and doubt.
As you turn your thoughts to love and light, you are not turning a blind
eye to what is before you.
Instead you are choosing to see past surface appearances, seeing the
Light of Divine Source within each person.
How another chooses to see, feel, or act is not yours to judge.
We say this to you ... choose how you shall travel the path before you.
You are protected always, enfolded in love and light, given courage and
strength to do what needs to be done.
We do not say you must stay where you are, surrendering to the will of
others.
We are saying travel with love and light, practice mercy upon yourself
and others. Accept where you are, keeping your eye on where you want
to be.
Be kind and loving this day.
Mercy shall accompany you all your days.

Day 238

FAITH IS ...
Angel of Faith

Faith is the belief in the unknown.
Faith is the belief in the unseen.
Faith is the belief in the un-proven.
Faith is a sense of knowing what is for our own highest and best good.
Faith is knowing which fork in the road to take.
Faith is a cloak of belief in the power within and that of my brethren and me.
Faith is surrendering the fear of lack.
Faith is surrendering the fear of being alone, being lonely, not finding or being with one who loves you unconditionally.
Faith is surrendering dis-ease of the body, the mind, the heart, of the Spirit.
Faith is trusting that which you know to be your truth.
Faith is having strength and courage to do what must be done in the light of day.
Faith is knowing when to stay the course and when to step out past all you have ever known, knowing there will be something to step upon or you will be given wings to fly. Faith is knowing you are Divinely protected in times of great pain, indecision.
Faith is knowing all is well.
Faith is trusting your inner guidance and acting upon it.
Faith is .....

Day 239

FLAMES OF PURIFICATION
Archangel Michael

Open your hands facing the heavens, cupping them together.
Lay all your burdens in your open hands.
Imagine all you wish to release, to move through, all that is not of love
and light in your heart, mind, soul and Spirit to be in your hands.
Feel the weight of all you carry in your hands, now this moment.
Imagine a fire pit before you; the flames dancing before you.
Know you are safe and protected from all you have placed in your
hands.
No harm shall come to you.
The flames of the fire before you are open to receiving all you wish to
release, to purify, to heal, to transform.
Imagine every thought, emotional wound, disappointment, fear of the
known and unknown being transported one by one into the flames of
the fire.
The flames dance and flicker, turning bright orange as it transmutes all
you are willing to release into the Light.
Feel you entire being become lighter and lighter, freeing you from all
that has come before. Feel your entire being become free from all you
have carried.
Feel you entire being sigh with relief for there is nothing that cannot be
yours for the asking.
Feel the warmth of the flames warm your Spirit, your body, thoughts,
your heart.
Travel this day in love and light for there is only love and light.
Be willing to step out from the shadows which attempt to bind you.

Step into the light beloved child.
Give thanks for all that has come before.
Give thanks for all that is yet to be.
Give thanks ...

Day 240

SEEKERS OF THE WAY
Hadraniel

~*~

In all things be true to you.
In all things speak with integrity.
In all things judge not lest you be judged.
In all things be kind to yourself and to all around you.
Place your physical and energy bodies into the Light.
Place all who seek to do you harm in the Light.
Acknowledge that which is before you step aside from all that is not of
Love and Light, allowing all to flow past you.
The way of Divine Source shall prevail in all things, in all ways.
The Light shall rise illuminating the path before you this day and all the
days before you. That which you seek shall be found.
That which is before you shall melt from you in the light of the dawn.
Seek that which is of love.
Seek that which is unconditional for all shall be revealed to you with an
open heart, an open mind, a forgiving Spirit.
Light a candle of white, light a candle of gold, light a candle of blue.
All is made whole in the light.
Step into the Light forsaking all that is behind you.
Step into the Light this day and all the days before you.

Day 241

BALANCING KNOWING AND RATIONAL REALITY
Angel of Knowing

⟨⁓⟩

A deep sense of *knowing* is that which is beyond rational reality.
Rational reality is all that you touch, see, hear, taste and smell.
Knowing is the intuitive voice, your gut feeling, a tingling sensation as
you or another speaks a truth.
Have you wondered or given thought to that which you *know* and that
which appears as *reality* in the world of matter around you?
Do you at times, experience inner conflict between that which is and
that which you *know* to be a truth?
How does one balance the Inner-Self with the outer world of physical
manifestation?
As you step along the path before you placing one foot in front of the
other, you begin to resolve the feeling or sense of separateness between
that which you *know* and that which is.
Be willing to see through the appearance of *rational reality*.
Be willing to trust your Inner-knowing.
Be willing to walk the path before you in the *light of knowing* all is well
with you.
Be willing to accept that which flows within you also flows through and
around you, balancing both your Inner-Self and the world of matter all
around you.
Be willing to open yourself to all you are now, this moment.
You are whole; you are complete traveling the path before you balancing
all things, all emotions, all thoughts, all actions.
Be willing ....

Day 242

SEEK COURAGE WITHIN
Angel of Being

⌒✿⌒

Seek and you shall find. Seek and you shall be found.
Open your eyes to all that is around you. Are you what you see?
In part, you are what you see in all that has manifested around you.
Yet you are not defined by that which has manifested around you.
You are the essence of that which you desire to be.
You are the essence of that which has manifested as you draw unto you
all that you feel, think, and act upon.
You resonate from the heart, the core essence of your entire being.
Your actions speak for you, creating action all around you.
Detach from what could have been, should have been.
Attach to what is yet to be for in the bliss of living in the moment, all is
made manifest in love, harmony, joy, prosperity, health, happiness.
Seek courage within you causing new action, new thoughts, new
emotions.
Seek courage within stepping into the light of forgiveness for all that is
now behind you. Step into the light of knowing all is well, all is healed,
all is forgiven.
See, feel, speak, act differently.
That which is before you shall mirror your true Self.
Accept where you have been, detaching from all that has come before
bringing you to where you are.
Open your heart, mind, your Soul to all which awaits you in the Realm
of Spirit for it shall be made manifest.
Seek courage within; be willing to see differently this day.

Day 243

A DAY OF REMEMBRANCE
Angel of Freedom

⟶⟶

This day is a day of remembrance for all who have and continue to give
their lives for others.
This day is a day of gratitude for all who sacrifice for the dream of
freedom.
This day is a day for soldiers everywhere who answer the call to arms.
A soldier is one who answers the call, a call to be compassionate where
there is no compassion.
A soldier is one who answers the call to radiate the Light of Source
where there is darkness.
A soldier is one who answers the call to forgive themselves and others.
A soldier is more than one who bears arms.
A soldier provides comfort, compassion, healing, forgiveness, love.
A soldier answers the call of the Creator to stand and be counted.
There are many soldiers traveling many paths.
Express your gratitude to all who serve the highest and best good for all.
Be kind to yourself as you travel the path before you, having the courage
to walk the path before you.
You are a soldier, a soldier of Light bearing gifts of love, light,
compassion, gratitude, courage, strength.
This day is a day of remembrance of all who have come before you so
you may walk in the light in peace.
Celebrate the freedom to choose.

Day 244

WISDOM OF THE AGES
Archangel Raziel

⌇

All that lay before you is the physical manifestation of thought, emotion, desire.

All that lay before you is the physical manifestation of that which comes from love or fear.

All that lay before you is the physical manifestation of all that has come before this moment, bringing you to this present moment.

All that lay before you is the physical manifestation of who you were.

All that is yet to be made manifest in physical form is thought, emotion, desire.

Seek thoughts, emotions which serve your highest and best good.

Seek the light and love of Divine Source and that of my brethren and me.

Seek the light and presence of Divine Source and the way shall be made open to you. Seek the light; all shall be illuminated before you.

Seek the light, all darkness and shadow shall be cast aside.

Seek the light and presence of Source.

Shine forth this day, a beacon of love and light.

Listen, for all is revealed to you for the asking, for the seeking, for the knowing.

How shall you choose to manifest that which is laid before you this day?

Journey well, for you are loved beyond measure.

Day 245

EXPANSION OF THE SELF
Guardian Angel of Spiritual Growth

We are all one. We are all connected, interconnected one with the other.
It matters not the way of others around you.
It matters not the path which brought you to this moment.
Where you are now, this moment is all there is.
Where you choose to be, is yet to be made manifest.
This day, as with all days, you may choose to begin writing a new script
for your life.
The setting sun releases you from all that has come before the dawn.
The dawn of each day brings forth choice to begin again.
Begin with renewed faith, passion for all that is before you this day.
Trust, have faith all is working with you, not against you.
If there is someone or something before you this moment which is not
to your liking, simply step aside allowing that which is before you to
flow past you.
Embrace all things, all people, all situations in love and light.
We do not say to you, embrace and hold close that which is not of love
and light.
We encourage you to embrace all with love and light, releasing to the
light all that is not of love.
With each step along the path before you, there is an opportunity to
choose.
The choice to flow effortlessly with wind or against the wind is before
you this day.

Day 246

FREE YOURSELF FROM WHAT WAS
Angel Prince of the North

There is much to be thankful for.
There is much to accept; there is much to discard.
Imagine there are two baskets at your feet.
One basket is violet, the other is golden yellow.
In the violet basket place all that has come before which no longer serves
you, all negative thoughts, emotions, disappointments, hurts,
experiences.
In the golden yellow basket place all that has come before this moment
which is positive, loving, and joy filled.
Look at the two baskets.
Which basket is heavy? Which basket is light?
Which basket would you choose to carry with you?
It matters not how much you place into the golden yellow basket for it
shall always remain filled with love and light.
Be willing to see, feel or sense the heaviness of all you have carried with
you in the violet basket.
Allow all in the violet basket to be transformed with love, freeing you
from the heaviness of what was.
Your entire being is filled with light and love, healing from within,
radiating peacefulness, radiating harmony and joy.
Free yourself to float along the path before you collecting, adding many
joy filled moments to the golden yellow basket.
Do not fear for all is made whole in the Light of Source.
Free thy Self from what was...

Day 247

POWER OF THE LIGHT WITHIN
Angel of Power

Begin each day breathing in Divine Light.
Begin each day with a moment of silence, giving thanks for all your blessings.
Give thanks for all that has become before this moment bringing you to where you are. Are you willing to experience the power of light and love within you?
Are you willing to release that which has come before, making room for all you desire? Increasing the power within is as simple or as challenging as you wish it to be.
Gifting another with compassion, a smile, a kind word, a kind gesture ... all are simple ways to increase the power within you.
Forgiveness may be a challenge.
Are you willing to forgive others and yourself for wrongs real or perceived?
Be willing to open to the power within.
There is much to gain in forgiveness.
There is much to gain in radiating the Light of Source upon the path before you this day and all the days before you.
How shall you choose to increase the power of Divine Light within you this day?

BALANCE GIVING AND RECEIVING
Archangel Metatron

ↅ

Balance is bringing together your many layers.
Balance is bringing peace to your Inner-Self with love and compassion.
Balance is giving and receiving.
Balance is being willing to cleanse your Inner-Self, your emotions and thoughts.
Balance is being willing to release that which is behind you allowing that which is before you to be received with grace, light and love.
Balance in all things.
Balance your Inner-Self with all that is before you.
Be gracious in accepting gifts from another, a smile, a kind word, a kind gesture, a cup of coffee.
Allow another to gift you with unconditional love.
Be willing to gift another with unconditional love.
Judge not, for in judging another you also judge yourself.
In denying another the gift of light you in turn keep you in the shadows of darkness.
Call upon me and my brethren, we shall be by your side in the moment of the asking. Call upon all my heavenly brothers and sisters.
Be willing to love you.
Be willing to give to you.
Balance in all things; balance giving and receiving.
If you are unable to receive, you deny yourself the very gifts you are wanting to gift another.
Seek balance within, peacefulness shall radiate outward in all things.

HOPE IS ...
Archangel Remiel

ℳ

Hope is the well of eternal faith.
Hope sparks passion within.
Hope never surrenders trusting all is well, all is being made manifest just as you desire or better.
Hope gifts you with strength and courage to place one foot in front of the other along the path before you.
Hope provides comfort and solace.
Hope is a seed, when carefully tended with love, mercy and compassion bears fruit beyond your dreams.
Hope is the spark of Divinity within.
Hope paves the way for truth, faith, unconditional love.
Hope is.....

Day 250

IT IS SAID...
Camael

〜

It is said there is Heaven on Earth.
It is said the meek shall inherit the Earth.
It is said all shall be made manifest in the moment of the asking.
It is said there is justice, Divine Justice for all who shall seek the Light.
To be meek is to be humble for there is no need to shout your beliefs,
the ways of light, for shadow and darkness shall be revealed in the Light.
Turning the other cheek is forgiving you, to forgiving others.
Turning the other cheek is not re-tracing steps which cause you harm.
Reach deep within; there is much strength, much courage to accept that
which cannot be altered in physical form.
Reach deep within, be at peace with all that is before you.
You are not alone in your quest for peace and harmony.
Heaven can be found in even the darkest of corners if you will but open
your eyes to see. Heaven is a state bliss.
Bliss is the space in between breaths, in between thoughts, in between
heart beats.
It is said there is Heaven on Earth.
Are you willing to see beyond that which is?

Day 251

LISTEN TO YOUR INNER VOICE
Archangel Uriel

Listen to your Inner-Voice.
All you crave is within you now.
Listen to the still small voice within.
Be willing to hear, to see with love in your heart.
Words become action.
Your actions or non-action become your trademark in the physical realm.
In the Realm of Spirit all is made whole, all is forgiven, all is healed, all is made manifest before you.
Listen with your heart. Listen with your Soul.
Listen, open your eyes seeing, watching all around you.
Are you willing to travel the path before you with an open heart, an open mind?
Are you willing, truly willing to be where your path leads you?
We do not say to you have no choice for all is pre-destined.
We ask if you are willing to choose a path filled with love, light, mercy, compassion.
Are you willing to accept a life filled with peace, joy, happiness, harmony?
My brethren and I seek only to serve your wishes, wishes for your highest and best good, to guide you, to protect and love you without condition.
Listen for we speak with you often.
Listen for we speak with love.
Listen ...

Day 252

REMEMBER WHO YOU ARE
Archangel Zadkiel

〜

You are a child of light.
You are a child of love.
You are a child of infinite possibilities.
You are a child created in the likeness of Divine Source.
How then can you deny yourself love, light, compassion, mercy, grace,
joy, harmony, peace?
Open your heart, mind, body, and Soul to all things.
Open your energy bodies to limitless supply of health, wealth,
knowledge, forgiveness aligning you with Divine Source.
You are more than your thoughts.
You are more than your emotions.
You are limitless for there are no limits in the Realm of Spirit.
There is no separation in the Realm of Spirit.
You are always connected with the Divine.
Go within; seek solace within your Inner-Essence.
Remember who you are.

Day 253

STATE OF GRACE
Ana'el

⌒✳⌒

Allow a state of grace to flow within, around and through you this day.
What is a state of grace?
Grace is stepping aside when it matters not what is before you.
Grace is allowing another to seek their path, not the path you would
choose for them. Grace is forgiving you for missteps along the way.
Grace is accepting the decisions of another whether or not they please
you.
Grace is being gentle with yourself as you travel the path before you.
Grace is compassionate, nurturing.
Grace is love, being open to seeing the Light within.
Grace is being open to seeing the Light within others regardless of
appearances, regardless of actions.
Grace is ....

Day 254

EXPANSION
Archangel Haniel

_ᴍ_

There is a knowing deep within you, a knowing that all is well, all is in
Divine Order. There is much change occurring all around you.
There is much change occurring within you.
Change need not be feared, for in change there is expansion beyond the
limitations of what was.
Expansion is growth, emotional healing, seeing, hearing, and feeling
differently. Expansion is being open to all that awaits you.
Expansion is being willing to shed all that no longer resonates within
your heart, mind, Soul.
Expansion is accepting the path before you may not be the same for
another.
Expansion is loving, gentle, and compassionate.
Expansion is accepting where you are, where you have been, remaining
open to all that is before you this day and all that is yet to be made
manifest.
Walking in the light, being in the light, radiating light gifts thee with
grace, knowledge, gifts thee with humility.
Journey the path before you radiating light, radiating love, radiating
hope, radiating courage and strength.
Journey this day in peace filled contentment.

Day 255

MERCY, COMPASSION, GRACE
Archangel Metatron

≈≈≈

As you step out into the light of the morn, be compassionate for there are many who cannot see the light in themselves.

Be compassionate with yourself for you have also walked in the shadows of darkness.

Be merciful towards all who have no mercy for themselves or others.

Be in a state of grace, be compassionate, be merciful; for all creatures great and small are beings of Light.

Be willing to see past the shadows of darkness within your heart center.

Be willing to see past the shadows of darkness in all who walk beside you.

Allow the Light Divine Source to shine through you this day and all your days.

Mercy, compassion, grace .... How shall you tread upon the path before you this day?

Day 256

BALANCE ALL THAT YOU ARE
Archangel Raguel

Balance all that you are, all that you have, with all you desire.
Balance that which is, with all that is before you.
Balance your Inner-Self with outer manifestation.
Balance hope with faith.
Balance your thoughts with all that is yet to be made manifest in
physical form.
Balance creates harmony.
Harmony is the manifestation of balance in all things, in your entire
physical and ethereal bodies.
Light a white candle, give thanks for all that has manifested within and
around you.
Give thanks for all is before you.
Give thanks for you are loved beyond measure.

Day 257

DIVINITY WITHIN
Archangel Taharial

⁓ᴍ⁓

Light a candle of white, allow the warmth of the flame to re-ignite the
Spark of Divinity within your core essence.
You are light. You are love. You are Divine Grace. You are perfection.
You are whole and complete, now this moment.
Allow the light from the flame of the candle to cast its glow all around
you, enfolding your entire being in Heavenly white light.
All creatures great and small carry within the Spark of Divinity.
Are you willing to see the Spark of Divinity within you?
Are you willing to look beyond physical realm limitations, seeing the
Spark of Divinity in all faces, all places, in all situations?
Allow the Divine within you to connect more fully with Divine Source
Energy.
Allow your core essence to shine through the shadow of darkness,
illuminating the path before you.

Day 258

BELIEVE IN YOUR SELF
Liwet

Many thoughts, desires, passions, adventures await you.
Perhaps there is one desire or passion which seems to be "floating" in and out of your thoughts, in and out of your awareness.
For a few moments, be willing to take a journey ... journey into your thoughts, your emotions surrounding the desire within you.
For a moment, allow your conscious mind to explore what it would be like to be living, breathing, feeling your desire.
Allow my brethren and me to assist you in creating your life the way you wish it to be. Believe it can be so and it shall come to pass.
Believe it shall not ever happen and it shall not.
We ask you keep an open mind to how all shall come to be.
We ask you be willing to open your heart, or perhaps expand your openness, creating a vacuum for all you desire.
Believe is shall be and it shall be.
Have faith, trust that all is indeed being made manifest for you as you desire it to be or better.
Believe.....

Day 259

TRANSFORMATIONAL HEALING
Archangel Raphael

⌒✳⌒

Beloved child, you are filled with love.
You are loved unconditionally.
You are cared for unconditionally.
You are guided without reservation.
Seek the light within.
Seek the Flame of Divinity within your heart center.
Seek peace and harmony.
Shed all that no longer applies, no longer serves your highest and best good.
Shed tears of joy, for all is forgiven.
Shed tears of thanksgiving for all is before you.
Step into the Light of Divine Source ... you are wrapped in Angel Wings of Golden Light. Be comforted for all is well this day.

Day 260

HONOR YOURSELF
Archangel Gabriel

Free you from the bondage of doubt, worry, fear of the unknown.
Free you from self-made conflict.
Free yourself, speaking your truth.
There are many blessings before you.
Countless blessings brought you to where you are now, this moment.
True, you have experienced much that was not to your liking.
Is there not even one golden nugget in all that has come before to be
counted as blessings?
This moment gifts thee with an opportunity to begin anew, new
choices, renewed faith, trust in the Divine, believe in you
Be unafraid to speak that which is within.
Be unafraid to love and be loved.
Be unafraid to be loved and to love.
Be unafraid to gift another as you would gift yourself.
Be unafraid to gift yourself as you would gift another.
Be fearless ... honor you this day and all your days.

Day 261

LIGHT OF DIVINE GRACE
Guardian Angel of Service

It is time beloved child to accept *being of service* also means being able to accept assistance from others where once there was none.

Being of service is not always about the giving of you to others unconditionally. *Being of service* is also about being able to accept that which others are willing, ready and wanting to gift you unconditionally. *Being of service* is being open to accepting gifts of service from others who have found a desire to be of service where once there was none. Graciously accepting gifts of service from another is *being of service*. Be willing to gift another by accepting that which is being offered you. *Being of service* is giving of thy Self unconditionally. Shine the Light of Divine Grace this day accept gifts of service being offered to you.

Go in peace.

All is well this day.

Day 262

YOUR GARDEN OF SPIRIT
Ra'amiel

～※～

Compassion is the seed of your Soul.
Mercy is the seed of your thoughts, your emotions.
Loving kindness is the seed of your heart.
Compassion, mercy, loving kindness is the seed of your actions.
Many seeds have been planted with each step along the journey.
There are many types of seeds; seeds of discontent, seeds of desire, seeds
of lack, seeds of faith; seeds of love, seeds of judgment, seeds of empathy,
seeds of mercy, seeds of pity, seeds of joy.
The garden of your Spirit is tended with love, light, forgiveness,
understanding, acceptance.
To accept you is to accept others.
To accept others is to accept you.
One cannot express love for another without first loving themselves.
Do you speak words of unkindness to you?
How then can you speak lovingly to others?
We do not ask you to turn a blind eye to that which is around you.
We ask you acknowledge that which is around you choosing to see past
surface appearances.
See the Garden of Spirit within each living creature great and small.
Tend your garden with loving care.
How shall you choose to tend your Garden of Spirit this day?

Day 263

PURE IN HEART, PURE IN THOUGHT
Ha'amiah

⌒⁂⌒

The path before you is illuminated with Divine Light.
The path before you is filled with choice.
The path before you is a wonderland of peace, joy, contentment,
abundance and prosperity, love and compassion.
The path before you unfolds with each step in ways unimaginable.
What is it you seek?
Do you seek to expand your sense of worth?
Perhaps you seek your own Spiritual truths, gaining a better understand
of your life's purpose.
What so ever you shall seek, be pure of heart.
Seek for the gift of knowledge for yourself.
Seek for the gift of sharing the Light and Love of Divine Source.
Child of light, it matters not the name by which you refer to the Source
of All There Is. Seek and you shall find.
Ask and it shall be given.
Knock and the door shall be opened before you.
Choose wisely, choose from the heart.
Speak with love and compassion.
Be kind to you and to others, for there is no greater gift than
compassion.

Day 264

YOU ARE ...
Archangel Michael

Beloved Child of light and love, no harm shall come to you this day.
You are loved, protected, guided beyond your knowing.
None can touch you except by words or deed if you but allow shadow
and darkness to cloud your sight.
Breathe deeply the pureness of the driven snow.
Release the shadows that seek to overtake you.
Breathe deeply the pinks and blues of the morning skies.
Release the shadows of what was.
Breathe deeply the oranges and yellows of the night sky for they cleanse
all in your path. Release all that is not of love and light for you are
protected from all that is not of love. You are protected from all that is
not light.
There is no-thing, no one to fear except fear itself.
Look yourself in the eye; see all that is before you.
See love, for you are love.
See light, for you are light.
See strength, for you are strength.
Step into the Light of Divine Source.
All is revealed in the light for there are no shadows in which to hide.
Step into the golden yellow rays of light; allow the light within you to
illuminate all before you.
All is well with you this day.

Day 265

RADIANT LIGHT WITHIN
Azrael

—✦—

Be pure of heart.
Be pure of Spirit.
Be pure of thought.
In all things be gracious, compassionate, loving.
In all your thoughts be forgiving towards you and others.
There are many paths along the journey.
There are many choices before you.
Choose wisely, choice creates new opportunities.
Choice creates the opening of doors.
Choice closes doors to all that is behind you.
Step through the door of transition from all that has come before.
Step into the open door which awaits you.
That which is before you, waits to gift you with unconditional love;
pure radiant light. Light candles of white and amethyst purple.
The flame of the candles illuminates all, reveals all in golden light.
Imagine golden light within you; imagine golden radiant light warming
your physical body, your Aura, your entire being.
See yourself within a bubble of golden light this day, you are a beacon of
light in the darkness.
Be not afraid for all is well with you.

Day 266

GIFT YOURSELF FROM WITHIN
Uzziel

Power lies within you.
Empowerment is power of the Self and for the Self.
Power is not to be confused with becoming powerful, boastful, power over others.
Power is strength, hope, faith to walk the path before you.
There are many who seek to destroy the light within you.
You and you alone are capable of dimming the light which radiates from within you.
Call upon me and my brethren to stand with you, beside you, in front and in back you. We are always with you in times of joy, times of sadness, times of uncertainty.
Be merciful with yourself as you journey along the path before you.
Many gifts await you.
Many gifts are yours for the asking.
In so giving you also receive.
Gift another with the grace of mercy and compassion.
Gift yourself with the grace of mercy and compassion.
Gift yourself this day.
Rejoice beloved child of light for you are loved beyond measure.

Day 267

FAITH SIMPLY IS
Angel of Faith

Faith is a belief in the unseen.
Faith is a belief in that which is unspoken.
Faith is a belief in that which is unheard in the physical realm.
Faith lovingly wraps around your entire being in times of doubt or fear.
Faith lovingly protects you, strengthening your choice to move forward.
Faith endures when all else appears to have fallen away from you in
times of strife.
Faith is knowing all is well; occurring in Divine Time.
Faith is knowing there is a power greater than yourself gently guiding
your footsteps along the path before you.
What is before you this day ... be willing to reach deep within, re-
connecting with your Inner-Divinity.
Transition brought you to where you are, transition shall guide you to
all that awaits you in the days ahead.
Reach beyond what is known; be open to all which awaits you.
Walk in peace this day for all is well with you.

TAPESTRY OF YOUR LIFE
Archangel Jehudiel

Begin again this day stepping into the Light upon the path before you.
This day as with all days is a new beginning, releasing all your cares,
worries of the day and night before.
All is made fresh with each breath.
All is made pure by the light of the moon.
All is made whole in the light of day.
You are whole, complete, perfect now this moment.
You are a reflection of all that has come before bringing you to this time
and place, to this moment.
If you wish, take a few moments observing, remembering where you
have been.
Have there not been many blessings?
Have there not been many adventures, surprises along the way?
How many paths have crossed your own?
How many lives have you touched along the journey?
How many have touched your life as you journey the path before you?
The tapestry of your life is a beautiful work of art.
Appreciate the beauty all around you.
Be willing to seek the beauty of perfection within you.
Be willing to be a beacon of light, illuminating all before you this day.
Be willing to begin again.

Day 269

OUT OF THE WILDERNESS
Archangel Metatron

Lead me not into temptation ... lead me out of the wilderness of chaos
and confusion.
Beloved child you are where you are in this moment.
Look within, call upon me and my brethren to calm your fears, to
soothe your aching heart, to heal your body.
Allow yourself to be healed, beginning with your inner core essence.
Your inner core, your true Self is pure light and love.
Thoughts of doubt, fear, lack ... thoughts not of love and light diminish
the light which radiates from within your beautiful Spirit.
Step aside; allowing all that is not of love and light to simply flow past
you this day. Breathe deeply. Exhale slowly. Feel your entire being release
all your concerns.
Breathe deeply. Exhale slowly. Feel a sense of peacefulness enfold you.
Step out of the wilderness of chaos and confusion within you.
Step into the light.

SEEING PAST SURFACE DISTORTION
Archangel Jophiel

⌒*ℳ*⌒

See all before you through eyes of love.

Be willing to see past surface distractions, which attempt to distort the light radiating within you.

The Light of Divine Source is ever present.

Reach deep within you bringing to the surface all that is love and light.

We do not ask you to allow the ways, the words of another to run over you.

Be aware of that which is around you this day.

Be aware of choices made, choices yet to be made.

There is much change within and around you.

There are many who suffer in the darkness.

There are many who seek a better way.

There are many who look to you for strength, for courage.

We do not ask you to take the burdens of another upon yourself.

We ask you to be willing to see the light in all faces, all places, all creatures great and small.

Call all upon me and my brethren, we are by your side in the moment of the asking. Become a beacon in the darkness for many look to you for hope, compassion, a smile gracing the path before them.

Be willing to past surface distortion.

TAKE FLIGHT
Trgiaob

～※～

Spread your wings, take flight beloved one.
There is much beyond that which can be seen in physical form.
There is much to see within you.
There is much yet to be made manifest in physical form.
That which you desire most is yours for the asking.
Are you willing to open your heart, your mind to all that awaits you?
Spread your wings, look beyond that which you think you desire.
Reach within; be willing to discover your truest desires without
limitation, without restriction.
It is time to release you from shackles of what was, what can never be,
hurt real or perceived, frustration, disappointment.
Lovingly release all that has come before bringing you to where you are
in this moment. Loving accept where you are, now this moment.
Look to the Heavens, look within your heart center, reach beyond what
is known, for all awaits you in the Light.
Take flight. Spread your wings this day.
It is time to take that leap of faith, embrace that which is before you.
Soar into the unknown.

Day 272

IN SO GIVING ...
Muriel

∽𝓂∼

In so giving, you receive.
What is it that you give to yourself or to others?
Services rendered without reservation, without condition come back to you tenfold. Giving from the heart without reservation does not suggest you turn a blind eye, a deaf ear to that which is around you.
Without reservation is giving, being of service without thought of payment in kind. Planting seeds of love and light are simply planting seeds, giving to another without expectation.
Openness in heart and mind allows you and others to choose differently.
Openness is the gift of grace.
All creatures great and small evolve; expanding in love's unconditional light.
Breathe the air, smell the sweet perfume of the many plants and trees.
Exhale all that is not of love and light this day.
Walk in peacefulness this day.

Day 273

HAVE COURAGE
Malahidael

The Divine within you is your strength to journey the path before you this day.
The path before you beckons to you like never before.
It is time beloved child of Love and Light.
There are many who seek a better way.
There are many who are blinded by the light which radiates from within you.
Do not be discouraged for there are many more who share the in journey before you this day.
There are many who seek as you seek.
There are many who walk the same path as you walk.
There are many who see as you see, hear as you hear.
There are many who speak as you speak.
Have courage for all is well with you this day.

Day 274

WALK THIS DAY IN GRACE
Domiel

⌒*⌒

Walk this day in grace.

Walk this day with love in your heart; speak lovingly to your Self and to others.

Walk this day in the Light of Divine Source for all is illuminated before you.

That which is before you cannot harm you.

That which is before you is but a pebble beneath your feet.

That which is before you shall soon be behind you.

There is much to be grateful for.

There is much before you; be willing to see beyond.

Allow the light within to shine forth in all its glory.

The Light of Divine Source shall not be extinguished.

The light within is ever expanding, shining brightly as a beacon in the darkness.

Allow the light within to shine upon your footsteps this day and all the days before you. Walk in grace this day.

Day 275

WORDS SPOKEN
Hashmal

Energy is everywhere in everything.
Energy is sound vibration, thought, action, emotion.
All creatures great and small resonate with the sounds around them.
You resonate with energy within and around you.
How do you speak to your Self?
Do you speak harshly or lovingly?
How do you speak to all around you?
We do not ask you speak in a manner which would cause you harm.
We are asking you to choose your words with care.
We ask you to resonate more with vibrations of love and compassion,
forgiving all that has come before.
Forgiveness is releasing that which no longer serves your highest and
best good. Holding onto old patterns, anger, painful memories, limits
your efforts to move forward. Moving forward is embracing the light,
shedding that which is behind you.
Moving forward is stepping out of the shadows of what once was and
into the light of what is yet to be.
Allow this day to be one of transition from all that was to all that is.
Choose words spoken with loving care, words once spoken cannot be
undone.
How shall you choose to speak this day?

Day 276

MELODY WITHIN
Teiazel

⌐✼⌐

Listen to the rhythm of your heart beat.
Listen to your inner voice, inner guidance, your intuition.
It matters not the name you call the wisdom within.
You are a melody of perfection, created in the likeness of the Creator.
Your entire being is an orchestra of melody and rhythm.
You are a musician, choosing pitch, harmony, accompaniment with your
thoughts, your emotions, your actions.
The melody within creates a resonance, a vibration radiating outward
into all you do, say, feel, and sense.
If the melody within is not creating peace and harmony, how then can
that which is before you be resolved in peace and harmony?
It matters not the choice of another.
It matters only choices you make for you.
Choices of others have no dominion over you.
Listen to the rhythm of your Soul.
How shall you choose to create the melody within this day?

Day 277

TRUTH AND CLARITY
Archangel Ambriel

⋯

What is it you seek beloved child of light?
Do you seek to speak your truth more clearly?
Do you seek new opportunities in job or career?
Do you know what it is you seek this day?
Take a few moments, light a candle of red or silver.
Declare your intentions, that which you desire most.
Be truthful with yourself, what is it you truly desire?
Perhaps you seek a love relationship, a harmonious working
environment.
Perhaps you seek a deeper connection with Divine Source.
Focus your thoughts, your emotions upon what you desire rather than
not having what you desire.
Focusing upon what you do not want brings more of what you do not
want to include negative emotions and thoughts of lack.
Turn your thoughts to giving thanks for all you desire; open your heart,
mind, your Soul. Clear your inner space; create space for all you desire
and more.
Speak your truth with clarity.

Day 278

LET THERE BE LIGHT
Hvare-Khshaeta

Let there be light this day.
Light a candle of white, illuminate all which attempts to hide from you.
Shine the Light of the Creator upon all your thoughts, all emotions.
Be willing to see that which strives to hide from your inner sight, your
inner knowing. All is illuminated in the light; there are no shadows in
the light.
Look upon all people, all thoughts, all situations that would cast
shadows upon you with love, acceptance, forgiveness.
Surrender all which has become illuminated.
Surrender thoughts of lack, loneliness, fear based emotions.
Accept where you are, look to where you desire to be.
The Light of the Creator shall guide your footsteps along the path
before you.
Let there be Light this day.

CELEBRATE THE MOMENT
Emmanuel

∽*∾*∽

In peace there is joy.
In peacefulness there is bliss.
In Joy there is happiness, cause for celebration.
In bliss there is a sense of calm, all is well.
Celebrate where you are.
Celebrate where you have been.
Celebrate all that has come before this moment.
All that has come before has brought you to where you are.
All that is, shall deliver you to where you are to be in the days ahead.
How shall you choose to travel the path before you?
Do you choose joy and happiness or despair?
Do you choose abundance and prosperity or lack?
Do you choose peace and harmony or chaos?
Celebrate all you are, for you are a reflection of the Divine Spark within.
Celebrate the moment in all its splendor, for it shall grace you
differently in the next moment and the next.
How shall you choose to celebrate the moments before you this day?

RELEASE YOUR CARES AND WORRIES
Cassiel

Be not a beast of burden to your troubles, worries or concerns.
Become instead a beacon of light, for all is revealed in the moment of
the asking.
Be clear about that which you seek answers.
Be willing to accept where you are now.
Be willing to see from a different perspective.
Be willing to open yourself to endless possibility.
Be willing to accept change, accepting that which cannot be changed.
Be willing to forgive and forgive again; un-forgiveness harms only you.
Radiate light and love from your inner core essence.
Radiate forgiveness to all who have wronged you, whether it is real or
perceived.
Release all that no longer serves you.
Light a candle of deep amethyst purple, write or speak aloud to those
who have wronged you as if they are in front of you.
Your heartfelt words travel on the flame of the candle, releasing all that
is behind you.
Feel your shoulders, your entire being sigh with relief.
Feel or sense serenity flow through your physical body and that of your
Aura and your entire being.
Be willing to release your cares this day.

Day 281

LOVE IS
Theliel

⌒⋔⌒

Love is all there is.
Love is all encompassing.
Love is forgiveness.
Love is unconditional.
Love is seeing past surface appearances.
Love is grace.
Love is harmony and balance.
Love is speaking truth laced with compassion.
Love is all these things and more.
Love is not binding another to you.
Love is fearless, trusting, supportive, communicating with loving kindness.
Love is commitment to the path before you, stepping lightly in the warmth and comfort of love.
Love is gifting you with kindness and mercy.
Without love, there is nothing.
Love simply is.
Know you are loved beyond measure this day and all the days before you.
Go in peace.

Day 282

FAITH IS KNOWING
Angel of Faith

Faith, is knowing all is well in the face of any obstacle before you.
Faith, is knowing all is occurring in Divine Time according to the
Divine Plan for your life.
Faith, is knowing you have the choice to rise above any concerns or
worries.
Faith, is knowing you are loved, protected from adversity.
Faith, is knowing you have free will, choosing how to react to all that is
before you. Faith, is knowing you can call upon my brethren and me at
any moment to help you, we shall be by your side in the moment of the
asking.
Faith, is rising above the chaos of others around you.
Faith is .....

Day 283

ARE YOU WILLING TO SEE?
Paschar Angel of Vision

⌒*⌒

Seeing beyond physical appearances is a challenge.
Are you willing to see past surface illusion, the mask which conceals the
Divine in you and in others?
Being willing to see past physical limitation, is in part, being aware or
acknowledging that which is before you and choosing to see, to
acknowledge the Divine Spark within.
It matters not the outer layers, when the mask is so closely held.
Are you willing to see the Divine in another?
Are you willing to see the Divine in you?
Sight is more than seeing all that has been made manifest before you.
Sight is seeing through the veil of deception, shadow and darkness.
Sight is being willing to see that which is perfect, whole and complete in
you and in all creatures great and small.
Seeing does not require accepting that which is not of love and light.
Seeing is a gift, a gift of choice.
How shall you choose to see this day?

RELEASE ALL YOUR CARES AND WORRIES
Jehudiel

Begin again for all is made new in the likeness of Divine Source.
Begin again; breathe in light ... exhale darkness.
Breathe in white light, exhale shadows of what was.
Breathe in the Light of the Creator, exhale all that no longer serves your highest and best good.
Begin again with each breath.
Begin again this day, the page upon which you write your life's journey is fresh.
The page before you is bathed in the Light and Love of Divine Source.
Gift you this day, release all your cares and worries lurking in the shadows.
Step into the light beloved child, you are loved beyond measure.
Step into the light, allow that which is whole, complete and prefect within to shine this day.
Wrap yourself in Divine White Light this day.
Wrap yourself love of Divine Source, for all is before you.
Open yourself to new beginnings

Day 285

BEGIN WHERE YOU ARE
Israfil

⚜

As with all things there is a beginning and there is an end.
The end is not the end of life, the end of strife, the end of all things as you have come to know them.
The end is another name for transformation, releasing old ways, thoughts, emotions. The beginning is not starting from the very beginning as if nothing has occurred. Everything you have experienced, everyone you have met along the way has brought you to where you are.
Each breath brings a choice; a choice to think, feel and act differently.
Each breath is a beginning.
Begin where you are, moving past where you were.
Transformation is the willingness to see things, people and situations differently.
Begin where you are.

Day 286

TRUE MEASURE IN ALL THINGS
Archangel Metatron

⟳

Balance in all things, in all ways.
True measure is the balance between Spiritual pursuits and physical realm manifestations.
True measure is the balance between the Divine within and the realm of physical form. True measure is balancing giving and receiving.
You must first give to you.
As your Inner-Spirit infills your entire being, your cup overflows, having more than enough of all things to give to another.
In seeking a better way, balance must be sought between moving forward and leaving that which has come before behind you.
In releasing that which no longer serves you, there is balance creating a vacuum or void. The void newly created, in turn creates space to manifest in physical form all your desires.
In giving, there is balance in receiving.
In receiving, there is balance in giving.
One cannot truly give without be open to receiving.
One cannot truly receive without being open to giving.
How shall you choose to create balance in all ways, in all things this day?

Day 287

DISENGAGE FROM STRUGGLE AND CONFLICT
Angel of Serenity

⌒*ᴹ*⌒

Disengage; withdraw your thoughts, your emotions from that which is not of love. Disengage; simply turn your thoughts to that which brings a smile to your beautiful, loving face.

In your mind imagine you are doing an about face, turning a corner, walking away from conflict, surrendering the need to be right or to be heard.

At times silence is louder than words spoken or actions taken.

Surrender the need to fight for yourself.

Surrender the need to be seen.

Choose to see, to hear; allowing all that is not to your liking flow past you in peace and tranquility.

We are suggesting you be open; simply do not play the game.

We ask you consider playing a game of speaking kindly or do not speak.

Act kindly, think kindly allowing another to create their own reality.

Peace and Tranquility are yours for the asking, for the choosing.

How shall you choose this day?

Shall you choose to disengage from struggle and conflict?

Day 288

CUT THROUGH ILLUSION
Zachriel

⌒✕⌒

Memories of what once was, memories of what could have been,
memories of what has not come to pass.
All these things and more are stored in your physical body, you Aura.
Each memory, pleasant or unpleasant is stored within your thoughts,
within your emotions.
It is time beloved one to release all that has come before which is not of
love and light. Release all your cares and worries for all shall be revealed
in the light along the path before you.
In the light, there is wisdom, grace, knowing all is in Divine Order
occurring in Divine Time for your highest and best good.
In the light there is clarity, the gift of seeing past illusion.
Are you willing to cut through the illusions which bind you?
Are you willing to see a brighter future which awaits you?
Are you willing to trust, have faith all is unfolding before you in
accordance for the Divine Plan for your life?
This is not to say all is pre-destined for there is choice.
You were given the gift of choice from the moment your life began.
There are many choices before you this day and all the days before you.
How shall you choose to cut through illusion, freeing yourself,
awakening the Spark of Divinity within?

Day 289

EXPANSION
Angel of Spiritual Growth

✒

Expansion ... what does this mean?
Expansion is being willing to step beyond your own pre-conceived
boundaries. Expansion is being open to experiencing new things,
meeting new people, changing jobs.
Expansion is willing to release that which is now behind you.
Expansion is accepting you in all your glory.
Expansion is accepting your own Divine Nature, allowing the Flame of
Divinity within to light the way before you.
Expansion is accepting not all will understand or want to understand
your seeking the light.
Expansion is accepting your inner transformation being made manifest
in the outer physical realm around you.
Expansion is all these things and more.
Expansion is knowing your thoughts, emotions your actions benefit not
only you but all those around you.
Expansion is knowing you need not speak; you need simply walk the
path before you in love allowing the light within to illuminate the path
before you.
Expansion is ...

COURAGE
Archangel Chamuel

Have courage beloved one; there are many who support you.
There are many who protect you from shadow and darkness.
Seek courage from within; the gift of courage knows no limitation.
Gift you with courage to speak, courage to honor boundaries, courage
to step into the light.
We do not ask you to bridge a wide gap or cross a bridge all in one
moment.
Begin with one step and then another and another.
Look behind you; with each step forward you are no longer where you
once were.
Look behind you once again, now you are on the other side.
All which sought to distract you from your path is now behind you.
Courage beloved child, there are no shadows in the light.
How shall you gift yourself with courage this day?

Day 291

HARMONY AND INNER PEACE
Gavreel

ᴍ

Inner peace is a state of bliss.
A state of grace can be found in the space between breaths, in between thoughts.
A state of grace begins with a slow, deep breath.
Take a moment, close your eyes focus all your senses as you inhale slowly.
Feel your lungs expand as you inhale deeply.
Feel your body, your entire being relax releasing tension and stress as you exhale slowly. Focus your conscious mind as you inhale and exhale releasing thoughts and emotions with a sense of peacefulness.
As you experience inner peace harmony radiates from within, projecting outward into all you do, think, say, and feel.
Where there is inner peace, there is harmony.
Where there is harmony, there is inner peace.
Gift you this day with peacefulness.

Day 292

GIFT OF SIGHT
Paschar Angel of Vision

There is much to see.
There is much to hear.
There is much to feel, to sense.
Do you see only that which is visible in physical form?
Are you willing to see past surface appearances?
Seeing past surface appearances is being willing to see the Spark of
Divinity within all creatures great and small.
Seeing the Divine within all living things does not suggest you open
yourself to that which is not of love and light.
We ask you open your eyes seeing that which is of love and light,
reaching beyond that which appears to be shadow or darkness.
In reaching past the veil, you acknowledge the Divinity within.
Be aware of all that is before you.
Be willing to see, to hear, to sense, to feel differently.
Gift yourself with seeing this day. See the colors of the rainbow in all
you do.
Speak with loving kindness this day.

Day 293

OUT OF THE SHADOWS
Archangel Ariel

⁓⁓⁓

To be lion-hearted is to express, radiate, projecting love in all things, in all ways.

Yes, we understand there are many who would distract you from your path.

There are many who delight in your struggles.

Do not return to ways which are now behind you.

Do not seek the destruction of another.

Seek instead to step out of the shadows of darkness, out of the valley of despair.

Remain in the light beloved one, for there are many who seek a better way.

Look to the light placing one foot in front of the other along the path before you.

Smile in the face of adversity for love is the way, light is your path.

Journey the path before you in peace this day.

Day 294

CLEAR THINKING
Angel Prince of the North

⌒⋔⌒

In any given moment there are a multitude of thoughts in your mind, a
multitude of emotions in your heart and in your body.
Each thought, each emotion carries its own unique energy vibration.
You always have free will to choose your thoughts, your emotions, your
actions.
In moments of turmoil, dis-harmony, remember to breathe.
For in breathing even for a moment, the body, mind and Spirit release
all they carry.
In the moment of each breath is the choice to choose differently.
Choose to give thanks for your many blessings.
Choose to reach for the next best thought, the next and the next.
Choose to reach out to a trusted friend in moments when soothing
yourself appears to be overwhelming.
Choose to re-focus your emotions; expressing gratitude for all that has
come before this moment.
Choose to give thanks for all that is before you.
Clear your mind, releasing sorrow and pain clearing the way for more
love and light to shine through you this day and the next and the next.
Release thoughts from what was, clearing your mind, your body and
your Spirit for all that awaits you.

Day 295

LOVING NON-ATTACHMENT
Satarel

⌒✳⌒

That which is hidden from you, from your sight is revealed to you in the
Light.
Be willing to step out of the shadows of darkness, stepping away from
the corners and alleys of all that is behind you.
Knowledge, discernment, peace and harmony are yours for the asking.
Choose wisely, for in choosing so sets the path before you this day.
Begin anew this day, choose to honor you.
Choose loving non-attachment.
We do not say surrender all your possessions or relationships.
We suggest you release the outcome of declared desires, accept paths
chosen by others with humility and grace.
Attach instead to that of unconditional love, peace and harmony, joy
and happiness. Allow all in your life the freedom to choose, the freedom
to experience for themselves. Love with an open heart, open arms.
Listen with open ears; hear that which is spoken and un-spoken.
There will be many who pass through your life.
Enjoy all that is before you this day, for this day shall not come again.
Beloved child, you are loved beyond measure.
You are honored, for you carry the Light of Divine Source within.
Travel this day in peace.

Day 296

RENEW YOUR SELF
Israfil

⟶

Begin again; renew your Spirit.
Begin again; renew your faith.
Begin again; renew your commitment to you and to those you pledged
yourself.
What is before you this day?
What is behind you?
What is yet to be made manifest?
What is to be released, creating space for that which is to be?
Look within; you know what resonates and that which does not.
Look around, look outside of yourself, that which is close to you.
Step out of your own way, clearing the path for all to be made manifest
in physical form. There is much to celebrate, much to be thankful for,
there is much to appreciate.
How shall you choose to step upon the path before you this day?

Day 297

IN THE LIGHT
Gadiel

∿

Take comfort in the light beloved child.
There is only light and love. There is only truth.
There is only that which lights the way before you this day.
Yes, there are fear based thoughts, emotions, actions.
Yes, there is shadow among those who attempt to cast falsehoods. You need dwell only in the light of the Creator, for in the light all is revealed to you and all around you.
In the light there is no place for darkness or shadow to conceal untruths.
Step out of the shadows into the light shedding all that no longer serves your highest and best good.
Step into the light allowing your Inner-Self to be made whole.
Imagine a white light cocoon surrounding your entire being, extending out 3 feet in all directions.
Only that which is of love and light is allowed to flow through your cocoon of brilliant white light, all else is deflected away from you.
You are whole, complete, and perfect now this moment.
Allow your white light cocoon to heal past hurts, real or perceived.
Allow the white light cocoon to show you the way.
Know you are loved beyond measure.
Know you are wealthy beyond your understanding.
Know you are a beacon in the darkness.
Know all is well with you this day.

Day 298

SIMPLY BE ...
Rachmiel

∽ᴍ∾

Be merciful, be kind, be loving; be patient.
Trust, have faith, believe.
Be all these and more with yourself.
Be all these things and more with all creatures great and
small.
Release all who have harmed you.
It matters not whether the hurt is real or perceived.
Release all who have harmed you with loving kindness.
Release yourself for all perceived wrongs having caused you
harm.
In all ways, in all things, simply Be this day.

Day 299

FEAR NOT
Archangel Michael

∽*m*∾

Fear not beloved child for all is well with you this day.
Fear not that which is before you.
Fear not that which appears to distract you from your life's purpose.
Fear not that which is unseen.
Fear not that which is seen.
Fear not the dark night of the Soul for you shall step once again into the light of the dawn.
Believe; trust all is as it is to be now this moment.
You shall emerge stronger, more light filled than you can imagine.
Step into the light for all is made whole in the Light of Divine Source this day and the days before you.
Go in peace.

Day 300

PATIENCE
Theliel

⌒*ᶲ*⌒

Be patient with yourself for there are many around you who support and
protect you.
Be patient for much is being revealed to you.
Be patient as you heal what once was and shall no longer be.
Be patient for all is occurring in Divine Time according to the Divine
Plan for your life. Remember beloved one, you are free to choose, to
flow along the path before you or stumble over many pebbles, roots, or
perhaps even branches which may have fallen during the many storms of
life.
Be patient for patience is a virtue.
Nurture your dreams with loving kindness.
Be patient as you heal what will never be.
Be patient.
Be willing to tend your inner garden with grace, love, tenderness.
Be patient.

Day 301

GIFT YOUR SELF
Archangel Raguel

⁓ᶈ⁓

Gift yourself with harmony and balance this day.
Gift yourself with knowing all is well.
Gift yourself with belief, faith, trusting all is truly well with you this day.
Know you are loved beyond measure.
Know your prayers answered in the moment of the asking.
Know you are guided in the moment of your seeking.
Know all is in Divine Order.
Know all is as it should be.
Know all is being made manifest before you, for it is already so in the
Realm of Spirit. Travel the path before you this day in harmony.

Day 302

COMFORT OF SOURCE
Sachiel

⁓

The blanket of Source covers you this day.
The Light of Source enfolds you this day.
Unconditional love and acceptance surrounds you this day.
You are wrapped in a loving cocoon of light and protection this day and
all the days before you.
Travel the path before you with a light step love in your heart and with
music in your Soul.

Day 303

IN THE SILENCE
Archangel Ariel

Light a candle of blue, focus upon the flame beloved one.
As you gaze upon the flame, feel your body relax.
All your cares, all your worries simply fade away in the light.
Your shoulders feel lighter, your heart freer, your thoughts quiet.
Do you seek guidance this day?
Ask and it shall be delivered to you.
Trust all is answered in Divine Time.
Believe the guidance you seek is given to you.
As you quiet your mind, your thoughts become still, soothing your emotions.
Simply allow the answers you seek to be gifted to you.
In the silence all is heard. In the silence all is revealed.

Day 304

SOAR AMONG THE HEAVENS
Anpiel

Take flight beloved one; there is much to see, much to do.
Take flight beloved one allowing your Spirit to soar among the Heavens.
On the wings of freedom seek that which you desire most.
On the wings of freedom allow all that no longer serves you to fall away from you.
On the wings of freedom there is no limitation, no doubt, no fear, there is no lack.
Soar among the Heavens this day, be free in Spirit.
Be free in thought.
Be free from that which seeks to bind you to all that no longer is.
Take flight, flow in peaceful harmony this day.

Day 305

COURAGE WITHIN
Angel of Being

⌒w⌒

Reach deep within for you are whole, complete this moment.
Be in the moment.
Be here, now.
Focus upon all that is before you.
Release all that has come before.
Look not to that which has not yet manifested into physical form.
Be aware of where you are in this moment, keeping your focus upon that
which is yet to be made manifest.
Balance that which is within with all that is around you now.
Balance thoughts and emotions creating balance in your actions.
Things, situations, desires may appear to be moving slowly, yet all is
being made manifest for the highest and best good of all involved.
Worry not beloved one for you are loved beyond measure this day and
all the days before you.
Reach within. Faith, trust, belief are the cornerstones of courage.
Step out into the light knowing all is well with you this day.

Day 306

RELEASE LIMITATION
Ohrmazd

⌒✎⌒

What binds you to thoughts of limitation, fearing the unknown?
Take a moment; breathe deeply releasing all thoughts of lack, releasing
any fears of not having all you desire.
Beloved child of light, seek love within.
Have you tended the garden of your desires, pulling any weeds, releasing
stray thoughts of fearful doubt?
Have you fertilized your garden of desires with loving thoughts, joy and
harmony? Release limiting thoughts, old wounds which bind you to
that which is behind you.
Release the fear of not having all you desire in your life; peace, harmony,
love, prosperity, clarity, kindness.
Release behaviors that bind you to what was causing frustration, dis-
content.
There is much abundance if you would but open your eyes to see, open
your ears to hear. Reach for the sky, reach for the stars, reach for all you
desire in your life, releasing limitation in all its many forms.

Day 307

DIVINE NATURE WITHIN
Guardian Angel of Spiritual Growth

⁓ɱ⁓

Be still this day, awakening your inner core essence.
Your core essence is your true Self, that which guides you along the path
before you. There are many pebbles, stones and perhaps tree roots which
attempt to trip you, distracting you from trusting.
Trust all is well occurring in Divine Time in-tune with choices made
providing guidance with each step, each breath, each emotion, each
thought along the way.
Be not afraid, do not focus upon the absence of what you desire to be
made manifest.
Be not afraid of that which awaits you just beyond the next bend.
All is well this day.
All is in alignment for your highest and best good.
All things are for your joy and happiness, peaceful harmony, serenity
and balance, prosperity and abundance.
Free yourself this day, discovering a new found peacefulness within.

Day 308

TRUST, BELIEVE, STRENGTH
Uzzah

⌒⁓

Divine Source does not seek to deny that which you desire.
All you desire and more is yours for the asking, for the seeking, for the knocking upon the door.
There are many variables, many degrees of wanting, of desire; just as there are many levels of Spiritual Expansion.
Appearances are deceiving, appearances flow along the surface, floating on the breeze called life.
Have faith, believe all is as you desire it to be or better beloved one.
For all shall be made manifest at your feet, in your heart, and in your thoughts into physical form or you shall no longer feel the ache of not having what you desire.
All is made whole in the asking, in the wanting.
All is made whole in the moment desire is conceived.
All is healed in the moment of the asking.
All is granted you for there is no-thing you cannot have, nothing you cannot do, nothing you cannot be.
Have patience for all is granted.
Trust the process; be true to you as all things, all desires unfold before you.

Day 309

CHOOSE GRACIOUSLY
Gamaliel

Do not doubt.
Do not Fear. Instead look within, look to the true essence of your being.
Your core, the essence of your being is filled with the light of the
Heavens.
Your core essence is rainbow light radiating outward, clearing the way
before you. Graciously allow that which has come before this moment
to simply flow away from you. Do not look back; look ahead to all that
awaits you with openness.
Gift you with clarity, the freedom to glide gently along the path before
you.
There is freedom in choice; choose wisely for in choosing you choose
judgment or non-judgment.
You choose love or fear.
You choose light or darkness.
How shall you choose gifts to receive gifts given this day?

Day 310

CHANGE
Samandiriel

It is said; change your thoughts and what you think about changes.
Choose to see differently and what you see changes.
Choose to feel differently and you will heal yourself and others.
It is not about healing others so you may heal.
It is about healing yourself which in turn allows another to heal.
Do you at times wish a "do over" to "rewind" an event or situation?
Perhaps you desire another opportunity to change a behavior or long
standing pattern of self-doubt or fear of not having all you desire in your
life.
Each moment is a gift; a gift to choose, to think, to feel and to see
differently.
If you are willing, choose an event or situation you wish to "do over" ...
breathe deeply, exhale slowly ... imagine how you would do things
differently.
Would you speak more kindly to yourself or others?
Would you look past perception seeing the Divine Light within?
Would you allow fear to overtake you or reach out to another to help
you through?
Your "do over" may or may not change what has come before.
Your "do over" may create a new opportunity with another to act
differently setting you free from what was.
Reach out to yourself; reach out to another releasing any attachment to
the outcome. Reach out this day; step into the Light for all is in Divine
Order.

Day 311

GIFT OF HEALING
Archangel Raphael

⌒✼⌒

That which is before you this day is a gift, embrace it with an open
heart, with open arms, open mind.
All that has come before this moment has brought you to where you are.
Where you choose to be in the next moment is a gift of choice.
Choose wisely for you are whole, complete and perfect now this
moment.
Imagine healing rose light weaving in and around your entire being,
flowing gently through your physical body, radiating outward into your
Aura.
Imagine healing rose light begin to wrap around you, forming a soft,
loving cocoon. Breathe in healing rose light, exhale pain and sorrow.
Know with each breath you release all that would keep you from
expressing joy and happiness this day.
Be willing to free yourself beloved one, resting your Spirit in love.

Day 312

RESONATE, RADIATE HARMONY
Archangel Jehudiel

⌒✳⌒

Harmony is a state of mind, a state of physical energy, a state of heart, a state of Spirit. Harmony is balance in all things in all ways.
Harmony is walking the path before you in faith all is well regardless of appearances, perceptions in physical form.
Create a sense of harmony within, the inner space within your core essence where all things spoken and unspoken become seamless creating a sense of bliss.
It is possible, for all things are made whole, complete and perfect in the moment of conception. Resonate, radiate, projecting harmony.

Day 313

EXPRESS GRATITUDE
Anauel

⌇

This day is a new beginning, as is each new day before you.
This day is a gift of peace, prosperity, harmony, love and compassion.
There are infinite ways to express and receive prosperity.
Prosperity is not measured solely in gold coin.
Prosperity is measured in the giving of a smile, a kind word, compassion where there is none, loving kindness when all else appears to be its blackest.
Trust all is well with you this day and all the days before you.
Have faith all is unfolding before you in ways not yet imagined.
There is much to celebrate this day.
There is much to release making way for all things desired.
In all things, in all situations express compassion for you and for others.
Trust all is occurring in Divine Time in accordance with the Divine Plan for your life. Choose wisely this day, express gratitude for all that is before you.
Express gratitude, for there are many blessings in your life now this moment.
Express gratitude this day and all days, all is well.

Day 314

PROPER MEASURE
Archangel Metatron

That which is balanced seeking the light of the Divine Flame within, sustains you.
In all things be balanced.
In all things be true to your inner essence of light and love.
In all things speak your truth not the truth of another.
In all things be compassionate.
Forgive you for all transgressions real or perceived.
In all things seek the light.
In all things speak with loving kindness for once spoken cannot be undone.
Proper measure is knowing when to stay the course and when to move forward leaving all that no longer serves your highest and best behind you.
Do not look behind you beloved one, look to the path before you for there are many glorious gifts which await you.
Go forth this day in peace, traveling the path before you in confidence all is well this day. Go in peace.

Day 315

SEEK THE LIGHT
Angel of Intuitive Illumination

Allow your Inner-Self to soar among the Heavens beloved one.
Allow your heart to be free from pain, hurt, disappointment, sorrow,
fear of lack.
Allow your heart to express joy, happiness, peaceful contentment.
Look about you this day.
Are there not many blessings for which to give thanks?
Seek first the light for there is much light and love for you.
How does one seek light and love?
Look first to yourself, your true essence is light and love.
In all things seek the ways of loving kindness, speaking with softness,
seeing the Divine Spark within all creatures great and small.
No matter the circumstances love and light shall prevail.
Step into the light, do you not see more clearly in the light?
Do you not feel more love in the light?
Why then would you choose to be any other place?
The Spark of Divinity within shines more brightly in the light.
Be not afraid, shed that which no longer serves you; embrace change for
it is the way of expansion.
Travel the path before you this day in peaceful harmony.
All is well.

Day 316

PURITY AND TRUTH
Angel of Mercy

⌒*n*⌒

Be merciful this day.
Be merciful with yourself beloved one for there is much before you this day.
Be merciful in thought, be merciful in deed.
Be merciful with others.
Judge not lest ye be judged.
Forgive first yourself, forgiveness for others shall follow.
Be generous; grace others with a smile, a kind word, a kind thought.
Be compassionate in all you say and do this day.
Express the Divine Light within with grace and ease.
Be willing to see beyond the surface of physical manifestation for many seeds have been planted in your name.
Seek your truth; speaking your truth from your heart center.
Seek first for yourself, all else falls into place before you.
Step around the many pebbles which seek to cause you to stumble along the path before you.
Dwell not upon what was, see beyond what is, to what is manifesting all around you. Seek and you shall find and you shall be found.
Ask and it shall be granted.
Knock and all shall be opened before you.
Seek that which is truth wrapped in Divine Light.
Step into the light for there is no darkness, there is no shadow.
There is only love and light all around you.

Day 317

IN ALL THINGS
Ha'amiah

∾ᴍ∾

In all things be true to you.
In all things speak your truth with clarity and loving kindness.
In all things seek the light for the light shall guide you in all ways.
That which has come before is no longer.
All that has come before has brought you to where you are now, this moment.
Look to the light beloved one for there are choices, decisions, much to be grateful for.
All that has come before attempts to weigh you down, attempts to distract you from where you truly desire to be, to have, to do.
There is only you which holds you where you are, no other holds you.
True, others may have contributed to the place in which you find yourself.
Look within accepting choices made bringing you to where you are.
In the light of the dawn all is made new, all is made whole.
Blame not others; blame not yourself for you chose as wisely as possible in the moment of the choosing.
Each breath, each beat of your heart; each thought brings forth new pleasures, another beginning. C
hoose differently for in choosing differently that which you choose manifests different choices.

Day 318

ILLUSION
Archangel Raphael

That which is seen is often part of the whole complete truth.
Many times that is which unseen holds more truth than that which is
seen in physical form.
Trust, faith, belief are the corner stone's to manifesting all you truly
desire.
Be aware of where you are in this moment, acknowledging all that has
come before. Allow all that no longer is to be behind you beloved one.
Look to that which is before you.
Look to the light, step out of the shadows shedding the illusion of all
that no longer serves your highest and best good.
Step into the light, feel the warmth of the sun upon your face, upon your
shoulders which no longer carry the burden of things long since past.
Who is to say that which is unseen is an illusion?
Perhaps that which is seen in physical form is the illusion.
You alone know yourself best.
Yes, reach for another to assist you along the path.
Be not swayed by the words of others. Be true to yourself. Shine brightly
this day illuminating the path before you one step at a time beloved one,
allowing all that is before you to manifest into physical form.

Day 319

ALL IS GIVEN
Archangel Uriel

All you perceive is now behind you.
All that once was, has brought you to where you are.
All that lay before your feet shall be revealed to you in the light.
All shall be made ready for you when you choose to accept yourself for you are whole, complete and perfect now, this moment.
There is nothing you need do, nothing you need change.
Simply be, for all is made whole within you now.
All is granted you in the Realm of Spirit in the moment of the asking.
Be kind to your Self, be gentle, be loving for all is forgiven, all is made whole.
Step into the light; allow all within and all which surrounds you to be transformed with grace and ease.
Step into the light beloved one, you are loved beyond measure.
And so it is this day and all the days before you.

Day 320

REJOICE!
Guardian Angel of Health and Well-Being

⁓⁓⁓

Begin this day giving thanks for the many blessings which surround you.
Choose to see that which is made manifest rather than the lack of what
has yet to be made manifest.
Choose to appreciate all you are, all being offered to you.
Choose to step into the light along the journey before you.
Step out of the shadows of darkness for there is love and acceptance,
harmony and balance, abundance and prosperity, joy and happiness.
Divine Source is your source for all things. Rejoice for there is much to
appreciate. Rejoice for you are whole, complete and perfect now this
moment. Rejoice; all is unfolding before you without delay! Travel this
day in peace and harmony.

Day 321

WITHOUT CONDITION
Gazardiel

∼✿∼

In the rays of the sun there are no shadows all is bathed in warm
energizing light.
In the night, moonbeams illuminate the Soul.
Whether day or night, find your way focusing upon the light of the
moon, the bright yellow-orange rays of the sun, your own inner
guidance.
Listen not to the small voice within your mind which seeks to cast
doubt, to cast shadow. Are you willing to listen to your Inner-Self, the
part of you which is free from distraction, free from doubt or fear?
Take a moment breathe in the light of the moon, feel the warmth of the
sun upon your skin.
Face that which is before you this day be willing to see past surface
appearances.
Be aware of all that is before you; be willing to acknowledge all that no
longer serves your highest and best good.
Be willing to see, to hear, to feel, to sense all that is truth your truth,
allowing no other to include you to distract you from your path.
Your path is not the path of another.
In the accepting of another without condition, you also accept yourself
without condition.
Is it not possible there are others who also accept you as you are without
condition?
Go now, walk the path before you in trust, in faith, knowing all is
unfolding before you without condition.

Day 322

TRUSTING FAITH
Archangel Uriel

⌒〜

Trust is seeking faith within, knowing all is in Divine Order occurring in
light and love as it is intended.
You are a reflection of the Creator's love.
You radiate the Creator's Light.
There are no obstacles to all that awaits you.
There are no limitations before you.
There is only love, there is only light.
Face the warmth of the sun; face the radiance of the moon.
Do you not trust the moon shall always be in the night sky?
Do you not trust the sun shall always light your footsteps by day?
Trust in you as you would trust in these things for all is made manifest
before you in light.
All is made whole in love.
Trust the light within expressing love for you and all around you.
It matters not the circumstances in which you find yourself in this
moment for all is conceived in love; light illuminates the path before
you this day.

Day 323

THE DIVINE WITHIN YOU
Zachariel

Remember who you are.
You are whole, complete and perfect now this moment.
There is nothing you need to do.
There is nothing you need to change.
There is only love.
There is only light.
You are Divine Love, Divine Light.
You are a reflection of all that is Divine within you.
Are you willing to radiate your true essence of light and love?
Are you willing to see the perfection within?
Are you willing to see perfection within others?
Judge not. Condemn not.
Gently remind yourself of all that has come before, releasing all that no
longer serves you.
Smooth the way before you, judge not yourself.
Clear your mind; clear your heart, clear your thoughts...remember who
you are.
Distractions
Sagnessagiel
All that is before you this day and all the days before you shall be
illuminated in light. Travel your path in peacefulness, allow not
distractions disguised as doubt, fear, or confusion to tempt you from
your chosen course.
There are many ways for truth, love, understanding and wisdom to be
revealed in the light.

Follow your heart, place one foot in front of the other, be aware, be open to all that is before you.

Allow that which does not resonate in love and light to simply pass you by.

Be willing to accept the gift before you with loving kindness.

Forgive yourself for thoughts of doubt, thoughts of fear.

Accept patience as your constant companion along the journey before you.

All is well with you this day.

Trust, patience, forgiveness, wisdom, understanding; how shall you choose to walk this day?

Day 324

BE AWARE
Camael

⌒⋙⌒

Become quiet, breathe deeply exhaling slowly; gift yourself with
releasing all your cares and worries.
Gift yourself with peaceful intentions filled with radiant light.
Gift you with loving thoughts, gentleness, with compassion.
This day is a gift to you.
Be peaceful, be gentle, nurturing you this day.
Be aware of your thoughts, your emotions, your actions.
Breathe deeply; exhaling slowly releasing all that is not of love and light.
Seek within you all you desire, become that which you desire.
Be love, be kind, be compassionate.
In the quiet be willing to see beyond that which is before you.
Be aware of where you are.
Be aware of all that has come before.
Be aware of all that is yet to be.
Be not afraid, breathe in radiant white light, exhale white light.
Become as a feather, flowing through this day with grace and ease.
Be aware.....

Day 325

WITHOUT LIMITATION
Pathiel

⁓

Light a yellow candle, focus upon the flame.
Feel your mind, your heart begin to open allowing all that is of light and love to flow through you without condition.
Allow you to release all that is not of love and light.
Open to all that is of love and light.
Open your heart, open your mind.
Acknowledge that which is around you.
Acknowledge that which is within you.
Be willing to see beyond perceptions, beyond that which has manifested into physical form.
Be willing to see, to feel, to sense, to hear that which is before you just beyond your physical sight.
Be willing to accept where you are without limitation.
Be willing to allow yourself the gift of manifesting all you desire in its truest form without condition, without limitation.
Be willing to travel the path before you in faith, trust, knowing all is manifesting without limitation.

Day 326

QUIET YOUR MIND
Archangel Sandalphon

⤳

Quiet your mind; quiet your thoughts, quieting the noise all around you.
In the silence, in the stillness all is heard.
Sit in the stillness, sit in the silence.
Allow your body, your mind to become still.
If you are constantly in motion, constantly in the noise how then can you hear your own thoughts?
How can you hear me or my brethren?
How can you hear answers given?
If there is constant motion, constant noise there can be only chaos, disharmony.
Quiet your mind beloved child of light; all is well with you and those around you.

Day 327

FAITH, TRUST, BELIEVE
Zuriel

⌒⋎⌒

During times of confusion, distraction, dis-harmony, uncertainty, seek
Divine Source. Look within, for there is hope, strength, faith, belief,
harmony, contentment.
There are many challenges all around you.
There are changes occurring within you.
All as you know it may be changing, transitioning before you.
It is understandable to be unsure of that which will occur in the next
moment and the next.
Be assured all is well.
Give thanks for transition, appreciate where you are, knowing all is
manifesting before you.
Be wise, be prudent, appreciate all you are, all you have, all that is gifted
to you.
Learn, appreciate, and move forward.
Do not allow the fear of others to cloud your inner sight, your inner
knowing, all is well. Look to Divine Source.
Know all is well with you this day.
Call upon me, I shall assist you in times of uncertainty, all is made
manifest now this moment.
Have faith, trust, believe.

Day 328

THE RADIANCE WITHIN
Archangel Uriel

~*~

You are a light, a brilliant light among the shadows.
Fear not the words of others.
Fear not the emotional untruths of others.
Fear not doubt, lack.
Fear not the unknown.
Choose to reach through fear beloved one.
Choose to reach through that which seeks to bind you to that which
does not resonate within you.
Reach through that which has come before bringing you to this
moment.
Reach through fear, be not afraid there is light, there is love, there is
abundance.
There is peace, there is harmony, there is prosperity.
Allow the radiance within you to shine more brightly, more clearly,
more lovingly.
Be aware, be prudent.
Choose to reach through fear.
Allow your inner light to radiate through you and before you
illuminating the path before you this day.
Remember who you are, a beloved child of the Light.

Day 329

ACCEPT UNCERTAINTY
Angel of Faith

⟶

Faith is knowing all is in Divine Order.
Faith is knowing all is manifesting as you desire or better.
Faith is believing all is occurring in Divine Time.
Faith is going within seeking strength, moving forward into the unknown.
Faith is accepting you do not always know when the next opportunity will present itself. Faith is acceptance; knowing when you come to the edge of everything you have ever known choosing to place one foot in front of the other knowing there are stones to step upon or you will be taught to fly.
All is well this day.
Have faith all is unfolding before you.
Have faith there are stones to step upon.
Have faith, accept uncertainty.

Day 330

CHOOSE ONE THOUGHT
Archangel Taharial

Clear your mind, clear you emotions.
Stress, thoughts of lack, doubt or fear cloud your ability to see, to hear,
to sense guidance given to you.
Choose one thought, acknowledge where you are.
Be willing to turn, to pivot your thoughts, your emotions to all you
desire.
If you could change but one thought, one emotion which would you
choose?
In the choosing all things change.
In the choosing, you set into motion the flow of unconditional limitless
love, limitless possibilities, limitless opportunities.
There are many doors opening before you.
There are no accidents, there are no mistakes.
Choose one thought this day ... watch all unfold before you.

Day 331

THE UNKNOWN
Muriel

⌒⋙⌒

The sweet smell of perfume delights the senses.
Birds singing, a soft breeze gently brushing against your skin, the
melodies of a stream all delight the senses bringing a sense of
peacefulness.
In moments of peace there is harmony.
In the moments of harmony the way is made clear before you.
The moment there is dis-cord a sense of unease or un-balance, stop for a
moment, remember to breathe.
Do you fear the unknown?
Breathe deeply; exhale slowly allowing all thoughts all emotions that are
not of faith, peace, not in harmony with your desires to simply float
away from you into the light. Allow yourself to be open to all that awaits
you, it is not necessary to know the outcome of all things.
Trust in the moment, keeping your sight on where you want to be.
Allow you to fully experience the here and now.
The unknown need not be feared, open your heart, embracing that
which is before you this day.

Day 332

BE WILLING TO LIVE IN THE MOMENT
Ambriel

Be willing to see beyond the moment.
Be willing to live in the moment accepting that which is.
Be willing to express faith, trusting all is unfolding in accordance with your heartfelt desires.
Be willing to release all fear, doubt, thoughts of lack.
Be willing to acknowledge all that has come before bringing you to where you are.
Be willing to enjoy the path before you with every delightful twist and turn.
Be willing to acknowledge messages given to you.
Messages may be whispers in the breeze, be aware; smile give thanks moving forward towards all you desire and more.
Be willing to live in the moment.

Day 333

REFLECTION OF YOUR INNER-SELF
Angel of Freedom

⌒*ᵱ*⌒

Behold beloved child of Spirit, there are many choices before you.
All you say, all you do is a reflection of your Inner-Self.
Your inner Self is love.
Your inner Self is radiant light.
Words, thoughts, emotions actions reflect your current state of being.
Choose differently; choose to speak loving thoughts, expressing
emotions, actions with love.
As you walk the path before you this day, choose differently.
Speaking your truth with loving kindness heals all.
Speaking your truth with ugliness harms all.
The meaning of all things expressed requires time to bear fruit.
In the days ahead choose wisely; choose with loving kindness for
yourself and for others. Rejoice in the fortunes of others, for they shall
also be yours.
Rejoice in the happiness of others for happiness is also yours.
Rejoice in seeing prosperity for prosperity is your birthright.
Free yourself from limiting thoughts.
Free yourself from all that is not of love and light, joy and happiness,
harmony, prosperity and abundance this day and all the days before you.

Day 334

EMOTIONAL BALANCE
Angel of the East

≈≈≈

Seek balance within.
Seek balance in physical manifestation.
Seek balance in expressing all you feel, all you experience.
Seek balance in your thoughts, expressing yourself with loving kindness.
Seek balance in all things, in all ways.
Acknowledge what you feel, sense, hear, and what you see.
You do not beloved child need to express that which is negative,
acknowledge what you are feeling, expressing your emotions in as
positive a manner as possible.
Call upon my brethren and me; we shall assist you in all ways in the
moment of the asking.
We caution you in repressing all within your body, mind, and heart.
We caution you in allowing your thoughts, your emotions to overtake
your truth.
For in truth you are love and light.
We gently remind thee there is only fear or love; there is only darkness
or light.
Look to the Light of Divine Source.
Be willing to step into the light away from the shadows of what has
come before.
Be willing to shed the old, accepting all is before you.
Seek balance within, balance shall manifest all around you.

Day 335

TEARS OF THANKSGIVING
Hadraniel

⁓✐⁓

Do not weep for things beyond your understanding.
Do not weep for what has come before.
Do not weep in fear of the unknown.
Instead beloved child, weep tears of joy for the horizon is much closer
than it appears. Weep tears of celebration for all is but a breath from
where you are.
Weep tears of gratitude for your many blessings.
Weep tears of love, love heals all.
Our words to you are not hollow beloved one; words are the conveyors
of good tidings. Our words are the conveyors of truth, light and love.
Trust the seen and the unseen.
Open your eyes for they are cleansed with tears of thanksgiving.
Open yourself to all that awaits you in the light.
Open your eyes open your heart; speak your truth with loving kindness.

Day 336

STRENGTH TO MOVE FORWARD
Archangel Gabriel

Speak your truth with integrity.
Speak your truth with loving kindness.
Speak your truth to thy Self this day.
What do you fear to speak aloud?
Do you fear others will forsake you?
Do you fear others will judge you?
Do you fear fear itself?
There are many changes before you; step into the light, walk the path
one step at a time. The journey before you is not a race to the end.
The journey before you is filled with grace, love, prosperity,
manifestation, joy, happiness, peace and harmony if you would allow all
to unfold before you.
Strength manifests in many forms, remaining quiet, speaking your truth,
stepping beyond that which is known into the realm of the unknown,
reaching out to like-minded souls of light, knowing when it is time to
release all that has come before opening your Self to all that is.
Strength is acknowledging where you are, knowing there is something
better, richer, kinder, more loving in the next moment and the next and
the next.
Believe, trust, have faith all is unfolding before you.

Day 337

SPEAK WITH LOVE ON YOUR TONGUE
Angel of Eternal Love

⁓✿⁓

Comfort and solace are yours for the asking.
Nothing is ever lost to you beloved one.
No one is ever lost to you beloved child of Divine Source.
True people, situations, experiences come and then they depart in one
form or another. Love is eternal for there is only love and light in all
things in all places in all directions of time.
There is only love, for without love there would only be darkness.
True there are moments when all appears darkest before the dawning of
the next morn. Does not the light always come?
Does not love always find a way?
How then shall this day not be filled with love, forgiveness of yourself
and others?
How shall you choose to greet the dawning of each morn beloved one?
Transition occurs in many, many forms.
It is said there are no mistakes only that which co-incides.
It is said when one door closes, another opens. It is said there is a time, a
reason, a season, a lifetime for all things.
These are indeed truths, be willing to see, hear, feel, and speak with love
on your tongue. It matters not what has come before, start now this
moment expressing love for yourself. Love shall radiate outward from
you to all around you.
Be not afraid, love dissolves all that is not of love given even the smallest
kernel of desire.
Be not afraid.

Day 338

SPARK OF DIVINITY WITHIN
Archangel Haniel

Inner sight, looking within, seeing the Spark of Divinity within all
creatures' great and small, is a gift you give to you.
For in seeing the Spark of Divinity within yourself you must be willing
to see past surface projections of others.
True, the flame, the light within some is dim, never the less it is there.
We are not saying to you beloved one, seeing past surface projections
means you do not acknowledge what is before you.
We ask you be willing to see past surface appearances.
We ask you be willing to acknowledge the light within all creatures great
and small.
Be willing to see that which is often hidden even within you.
Be willing to acknowledge all are of love and light.
Be willing to accept there are moments it will be difficult to distinguish
the light, the Spark of Divinity.
Know the Spark of Divinity is always lit, always visible should you
choose to see.
Be willing to acknowledge the Spark of Divinity within you.
Be willing to see into yourself this day.
Be willing to see the Spark of Divinity in all around you.

Day 339

THE LIGHT WITHIN
Guardian Angel of Spiritual Growth

The light within sparkles with delight as you begin to awaken along the path before you. The light within is as a beacon in the darkness guiding your steps.

The light within expands, becoming brighter as you heal all that has come before.

The light within becomes softer with each word spoken with loving kindness.

The light within gains strength with each practiced step, trusting all is well, trusting all shall be revealed in Divine time.

The light within is your constant connection with Divine Source Energy.

The light within is your connection to your Inner-Self.

The light within is always lit, it cannot be distinguished.

The light within dispels shadow or darkness.

The light within is ...

Day 340

STAR LIGHT
Kokabiel

Allow the light within to shine brightly as a star among the night skies.
Do not allow the ways of others to dim the light within you.
In the face of adversity, close your eyes but for a moment, breathe in
white light exhaling shadow and darkness.
Breathe in the light of Divine Source filling you with a sense of ease, a
sense of peace, a sense of serenity.
The night skies radiate peace and contentment, the early dawn brings
yet another beginning.
Be at peace, shining brightly this day.

Day 341

LIGHT OF THE CREATOR
Sachiel

⁓ᴍ⁓

The Light of Divine Source surrounds you.
The Light of Divine Source shines before you.
The Light of Divine Source radiates from within you.
The Light of Divine Source enfolds you in all ways.
You are a beloved child of light.
You are whole, complete and perfect now this moment.
You are ...

MERCIFUL WAYS
Uzziel

Be merciful in your heart.
Be merciful in your ways.
Be merciful with your words.
Be merciful with your thoughts.
All is spoken in love and light.
All is given in love and light.
Can you not do the same?
Can you speak as if your tongue were laden with honey, still speaking
your truth?
Are you willing to speak differently?
Are you willing to see differently?
Are you willing to be merciful with yourself and others?
How shall you choose to express mercy this day?

Day 343

TURMOIL
Archangel Chamuel

⁓

Prepare yourself for the days ahead.
There is much before you, much to explore, much to experience.
There is much peace, much turmoil, much transformation, much
harmony.
Turmoil manifests in many forms.
Turmoil may appear in the loss of a friendship.
Turmoil may appear in the form of a disagreement between loved ones
and friends. Turmoil may appear as the ending of a relationship or
transition from the physical into the Realm of Spirit.
Turmoil may manifest in any form at any time.
Call upon me and my brethren, we shall smooth the way before you.
Call upon me and my brethren we shall assist you in seeing beyond that
which is.
Call upon me and my brethren we shall assist you in restoring peace and
tranquility, harmony, loving compassion, prosperity and abundance.
There is no quest too large, no quest too small, for all are equal in the
eyes of Source.
Ask and it shall be given to you.
Seek and you shall find. Knock and the door shall be opened to you.

Day 344

BEGIN THIS DAY
Kabshiel

~*~

Begin this day knowing you are loved beyond measure.
Begin this day knowing you are free from days log since past.
Begin this day knowing all unfolds before you free of judgment.
Begin this day accepting that which has come before knowing it shall
not hold you back from your good.
Begin this day accepting the many changes all around you.
Begin this day accepting the closed door behind you.
Begin this day accepting many more open doors in front of you.
Begin this day by exploring the countless possibilities, creating unlimited
choices, manifesting into reality with each breath with each beat of your
heart.
Begin this day in faith, trusting all is indeed unfolding right before your
eyes.
Begin this day marveling in complete gratitude for the many blessings in
your life now, this moment.
Begin this day knowing you are loved beyond measure.

Day 345

GIFT OF GRACE
Archangel Haniel

✧

Grace is soft.
Grace is gentleness.
Grace is gifting you with kindness in the midst of sorrow.
Grace is uplifting you in the face of adversity.
Grace provides inner strength to allow all that is not of love and light to
flow past you; take notice beloved one and step aside.
Open you to all which awaits you.
Open yourself to all that is yet to be.
Grace nurtures your Inner-Self.
Grace is the gift of your smile.
Grace is forgiving even the harshest among you.
Grace is unconditional.
Grace is a moment of bliss.
Grace is eternal.
Grace is a gift to be shared with your Self and others.
How shall you choose to experience grace this day?

Day 346

BEING OF SERVICE
Guardian Angel of Service

∽ஜ∾

Being of service; in what way or ways are you of service to yourself and others?
Being of service is speaking and acting with compassion.
Being of service is offering acceptance for where you are in this moment and the next and the next.
Being of service is acknowledging that which is before you, choosing to see beyond appearances.
Being of service is forgiving all who cause thee harm, for in forgiving others you clear the path before you.
Being of service is forgiving you for thoughts of doubt, lack, fear in any of its many forms.
Being of service is offering a kind word, a smile, accepting assistance, offering non-judgment, offering light where there is none.
Being of service is allowing the closed door to remain closed with heartfelt gratitude. Being of service is giving of yourself, tending your inner garden of light.
You are whole, complete and perfect.
You are loved beyond measure.

Day 347

CROSSROADS BEFORE YOU
Angel of Mercy, Purity and Truth

The crossroads before you is nothing more nothing less; it is another
form of choice.
Yet it is all there is in this moment.
The place in which you find yourself is all consuming; consuming
thoughts, emotions, actions.
That which appears to be loss, rejection, the seemingly instantaneous
manifestation of consequences beyond your control is a blessing.
Our words may sound harsh beloved one, do not despair for that which
is before you beckons you to trust, have faith, express gratitude for where
you are for you shall not be long in this place of discomfort.
Look to the dawning of each new day bringing with it choice to start
again, the choice to forgive, the choice to move forward with grace and
dignity.
We ask you to be kind, nurture yourself in the days ahead for you cleanse
from you all that no longer is, clearing the way for all that is, and all that
is yet to be.
Not all which manifests is of your choosing or your actions.
Forgive, release, embrace all that is given you for in the acceptance you
flow peacefully along the journey before you.

Day 348

BALANCE, HARMONY, PEACEFULNESS
Camael

The pathway to bliss is harmony, balance, peacefulness.
Balance between work and play, action and rest, speaking and listening,
receiving and giving.
Harmony is bringing balance to all things in all ways.
Balance and harmony allow a sense of peacefulness within and around
you.
Divine Justice is balance, harmony, peacefulness. Bliss is the expression
of that which radiates outward, projecting a sense of calm, a knowing all
things are working for and with you rather than against you.
Not all things, situations, people arrive in calmness.
It is what you do, how you react or do not react to that which is before
you which creates harmony, balance, a sense of peacefulness.
How will you choose to create your pathway to bliss this day?

Day 349

COMMIT YOURSELF
Asaph

⌒*✿*⌒

Declare yourself, declare your desires, declare your intentions.
It is said the pen is mightier than the sword.
The written word is mightier than that which is merely spoken.
Speaking truth is part of the whole.
Are you willing to declare yourself with the written word?
Are you willing to center your Inner-Self with the outer, aligning your
desires with that which is for the highest and best good for all?
Are you willing to set aside your perceptions of truth?
Are you willing to cast aside all doubt, lack, fear of not receiving your
heart's desires? Are you willing to trust the process?
Ask and it is given you in the moment of the asking without delay,
without condition. These words you have been given.
Do you not trust that which is given you in Spirit?
There are many distractions, many twists and turns upon the path
before you.
Trust all is occurring in Divine Time in accordance for the highest and
best good for all involved regardless of appearances, regardless of
circumstances.
Commit yourself with the written word.
Are you willing to commit yourself this day?

Day 350

WHAT DO YOU SEE?
Shelachel

━━

To see is a gift to be treasured.
What do you see when you look around you?
What do you see when you go within?
What do you see when you look at where you have been?
What do you see when you look at the path before you?
What do you see?
Be still for a few moments, look into yourself.
Where do you wish to be?
Do you desire to put that which has come before behind you, releasing all things, all people, all situations which no longer serve you?
Do you desire to heal your heart, your mind, your body?
Look within; be willing to see for all is illuminated by the light of the moon.
The moon casts no shadows.
The moon lights the way before you.
The moon brings closure to all things.
The moon gifts you with transition from that which appears to be cloaked in darkness, gifting you with the light of a starlit night sky.
What do you see?

Day 351

CHOOSE YOUR WORDS
Melchizedek

⌒*w*⌒

Beloved one speak kindly to you.
Speak kindly to others.
Speak your truth with kindness, with love, with compassion.
Be not afraid to express that which needs to be expressed.
Be not afraid of another's reaction or non-reaction for in the end words
not spoken simply wither within your heart, your mind.
Choose your words carefully, in choosing carefully you honor you and
those around you. All things in all situations contain a gift of peace or
dis-harmony, of love or fear, of lack or abundance.
Words unspoken are gifts not given.
It is true some words are best left unsaid.
Those left unsaid create the opportunity for harmony, peacefulness,
forgiveness, compassion, healing.
Choose your words this day.

Day 352

PATIENCE, BELIEF, TOLERANCE
Cassiel

⚭

In all things be patient.
In all things believe.
In all things choose acceptance.
In all things there are blessings those which are evident and those which are not yet revealed.
In all things exercise trust; exercise, belief knowing all is unfolding before you.
It may appear all is slow in manifesting or just beyond your reach.
In times of doubt, fear of not having all you desire, breathe beloved one for all manifests in its time for the highest and best good of all.
True, it often appears as though your prayers remain unanswered.
Call upon me and my brethren to instill within a sense of peace allowing all to unfold with grace and ease.
Tolerance is accepting that which is in the moment it occurs all the while keeping your sight, your vision upon that which you truly desire.
Patience, belief, tolerance all are gifts when see through eyes of love.
Breathe, allowing all to flow through you and around you in loving kindness.
All shall be revealed.
Go in peace this day.

Day 353

FORGIVENESS IS
Sagnessagiel

⌒✳⌒

Behold this day of all days; forgiveness is the key to happiness, joy, peace, harmony within.

Forgiveness is the release of all that has come before opening the way before you. Forgiveness is the clearing of doubt, fear, lack, dis-harmony, dis-ease.

Forgiveness is releasing all you carry within, all you carry in your heart. Forgiveness is releasing all you carry upon your back, all you carry upon your shoulders. Forgiveness is releasing all thoughts of anger, hurt, disappointment, betrayal. Forgiveness Is.

Day 354

SOAR ABOVE THE ORDINARY!
Trgiaob

⚹

Do you find yourself doing the same things over and over and over
again?
Soar above the ordinary!
Be daring!
Reach beyond your comfort zone!
Change one thing, one behavior, one thought, one emotion and all else
changes with you.
Yes, it is easy to say the words, think the thought I want to change, I
want to release this, I want to forgive, I want to be judgment free.
Wanting, desiring change is the first step.
Be willing to breathe deeply, stop, observe, acknowledge, accept, moving
forward one step at a time.
Imagine an umbrella shielding you, protecting you from the sun or the
rain.
In the same way an umbrella gives you shade from the heat of the day,
imagine all things unwanted are simply flowing around you, falling away
from you.
Dare to be different!
Dare to be YOU!
Dare to soar above the ordinary!

Day 355

EXPECTATION
Archangel Uriel

~𝓂~

Listen to your inner voice, the voice of discernment.
Listen with your heart, your inner core essence.
Receive that which is gifted to you in loving kindness.
Release the need to know what happens next.
Release the need to know that which continues to unfold before you.
Be willing to move forward into the unknown, into the next moment.
Accept the gift of surprise, the gift of expectation of having all your
desires manifest. Receive that which is already yours.

Day 356

BE WILLING
Sachiel

⁓✳⁓

Be willing to step beyond that which is known.
Be willing to step beyond that which is safe.
Be willing to step in to the light.
Be willing to step out of shadow and darkness.
Be willing to shed that which no longer serves you, serves your highest
and best good.
Be willing to cover yourself in the Light of Divine Source.
Be willing to trust, having faith that all which no longer is has fallen
from you making way for that which is before you.
Be willing to step away from what was, stepping towards what is coming.
Do not be afraid for you are whole, complete and perfect now this
moment.
Be willing to expand your knowing, beyond your comfort zone.

Day 357

JOY IS
Caliel

Seek that which brings you joy and happiness.
Joy is one of many keys to living a stress free life.
Joy is music to your Soul.
Joy is laughter, harmony, a sense of peaceful contentment.
Joy is accepting this moment, accepting the many blessings, sharing
loving-kindness. Joy is allowing you to be at peace with all that you are.
Joy is taking a moment to follow a butterfly's dance across the garden.
Joy is breathing deeply, exhaling slowly.
Joy is sharing laughter with another.
Joy Is.

Day 358

GIFT OF CHOICE
Paschar

There is much to see.
There is much to sense.
There is much to acknowledge.
There is much to accept.
There is much to discard.
There is much to heal.
There is much to rejoice for all things, all people, all situations are
blessings regardless of appearances, regardless of circumstances.
There is much which is seen and unseen.
There is much love and fear.
There is much light and darkness.
The choice is yours each moment of everyday.
You have a treasured gift of choice.
You have a choice between staying in the shadows and stepping in to the
light.
You have a choice between forgiveness and anger.
You have a choice between joy and sorrow.
You have a choice between acceptance and denial. You have a choice to
heal or remain where you are.
You have a choice.

Day 359

BLESSINGS IN DISGUISE
Barakiel

⌐√ℓ~

That which you desire most is made manifest in the moment of the
asking in the Realm of Spirit.
The question then becomes how to manifest all into physical form.
Many times that which you desire is before you yet it is not recognized
nor truly wanted. You may ask why would I not want something I
desire.
Truth be told, you may feel unworthy, undeserving or perhaps you were
focused upon that which you do not want rather than what you do
want.
You are showered with a multitude of blessings each moment yet you do
not stop to appreciate that which is gifted you.
Do you acknowledge your many blessings?
Give thanks for all you have been gifted.
Express thankfulness.
Express gratitude.
Perhaps you have been gifted with an opportunity shrouded in shadow.
Take a few moments; be willing to see beyond appearances.
That which is before you may very well be the diamond you have been
seeking.

RANDOM ACTS
Muriel

Give of yourself to others.
Random acts of compassion.
Random acts of loving kindness.
Random acts are simple, powerful ways to be of service, opening your
heart to giving and receiving unconditional love.
Random acts do not seek gain.
Random acts do not seek fame or glory.
Random acts are given from the heart, no strings attached.
Random acts are filled with grace.
Random acts are filled with joy, the pleasure of giving.
Random acts of loving kindness gift the giver tenfold.
A kind word, a smile, all are random acts.

Day 361

DARKEST BEFORE THE DAWN
Archangel Haniel

In the hours before the dawning of a new day, before the dawning of infinite possibilities, before the final manifestation into physical form, shadows of fear may rise within creating the appearance of great darkness all around you.

Know it is at this moment when all would appear to be beyond your reach, the skies clear, rainbows manifest in places where there should be none assuring you all is well, all is indeed occurring as you desire or better.

There is nothing, no one to fear, for there is no loss.

There is only love. There is only light.

There is only manifestation into physical form that which has already been made manifest in the Realm of Spirit in your name.

Day 362

SEA OF SERENITY
Taliahad

⟶ ✦ ⟵

Beloved child of light sink not into the depths of that which lay before
you.
Float upon the sea in complete serenity.
Release all that would bind you.
Allow all to be carried away by the sea away from you.
Allow the water, the sea to cleanse and calm you.
Be open to all which awaits.
Be open to all you desire.
Be open to healing beyond your imagination.
Be open to surrendering the fear of not receiving your heart's desires.
Float in the sea of serenity, knowing all is provided.

Day 363

BREATH OF LIFE
Archangel Remiel

⌒⌒

Breathe the breath of life; awaken the Spark of Divinity within.
Hope is a thought of something better, a prayer unspoken, wish unfilled.
One must accept the call to action for without action there can be only hope.
Hope is a first step along the path before you, trusting you are following that which is before you with integrity, with faith.
Hope is a beautiful gift or it can hold you where you are.
Breathe beloved one for there is always hope of a better, more loving way.
Hope is a gift to be treasured for without hope there would be much shadow.
Hope is the spark of light within, seeking to light the way, clearing the path to that which is for your highest and best good.
Allow the light within to nurture hope into strength, faith, trusting all is unfolding before you in love and light.
Hope is a gift to be treasured.
Accept the gift of hope as you move forward long the journey.

Day 364

BE WILLING TO SEE BEYOND
Radueriel

Be willing to see beyond your initial perception, beyond surface
appearances.
Be willing to see beyond pre-conceived ideas of what another should or
should not do or say.
Be willing to see beyond limitations you place on yourself.
Be willing to see another differently.
Be willing to see yourself differently.
Be willing to see beyond that which is in front of you.
Be willing to see beyond that which is known.
Be willing to see beyond into the unknown.

Day 365

MAKE WAY FOR THE NEW
Angel of Love

In an effort to be open and to remain open to all that is do you
sometimes find yourself attempting to protect yourself from pain?
Pain whether it is physical, mental, emotional, or Spiritual all emanates
from fear based thinking and fear based experiences that no longer serve
you.
This we say to you .... shed the old ... make way for the new.
How does it serve you to hold onto to what has come before?
By choosing to hold onto that which no longer serves you, how will
wholeness come into being?
How will there be space in your heart, mind, body and Spirit to embrace
that which you truly desire?
Imagine you are a creature which sheds its skin transforming what was
into what is.
See, really see all that is no longer wanted, no longer needed, all that no
longer serves you, leaving your physical body, your mental, emotional
and Spiritual bodies NOW.
See the old as it is, gray and lifeless.
Imagine Divine White Light coming into your physical body, cleansing,
rejuvenating, purifying, healing all that remains.
All that remains is born of Love.
Love of self, Love of others without limitation for their wants, needs and
desires and for your own.
Love for that which has come before.
Love for that which is yet to come.

Love for and in this moment giving thanks for all that is now behind you, making way for all that you are, all you have always been and will be.
How shall you begin this day and the next?
How shall you truly open to receive all that is?

Connect With
ANGEL LADY TERRIE MARIE, D.MS.

ANGEL DREAM TEAM
http://www.angeldreamteam.com/

Sacred Angel Realms A Pocket Guide into Nine Angelic
Hierarchies
Amazon Best-Seller
http://amzn.to/28Qjh4g

COMPIMENTARY GIFTS

International Angel Gathering:
https://angellady.leadpages.co/angelgathering/

Dissolve Negative Energy: https://angellady.leadpages.net/free-report-
negative-energy/

Angels of Prosperity Video Course:
https://angellady.leadpages.net/prosperity-angels-opt-in/

BLOG
http://www.angeldreamteam.com/blog

FACEBOOK
https://www.facebook.com/AngelDreamTeam/
https://www.facebook.com/SacredAngelRealms/

YOUTUBE
https://www.youtube.com/channel/UC2TOHSWJ53K4fDD_bM9
H-xg

Printed in Great Britain
by Amazon

47770275R00219